YORK NOTES

General Editors: Professor A.N. Jeffares (*University of Stirling*) & Professor Suheil Bushrui (*American University of Beirut*)

Arthur Miller

THE
CRUCIBLE

Notes by Dennis Welland

B.A. (LONDON) M.A. (MANCHESTER)
PH.D. (NOTTINGHAM) *Professor of American Literature, University of Manchester*

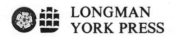

LONGMAN
YORK PRESS

YORK PRESS
Immeuble Esseily, Place Riad Solh, Beirut

LONGMAN GROUP UK LIMITED
Longman House, Burnt Mill, Harlow,
Essex CM20 2JE, England
Associated companies, branches and representatives
throughout the world

First published 1980
Thirteenth impression 1993

ISBN 0-582-02259-2

Produced by Longman Singapore Publishers Pte Ltd
Printed in Singapore

Contents

Part 1

Introduction

Miller's early life and career

The author of *The Crucible* was born in Manhattan, New York City, on 17 October 1915, the second son of a ladies' clothing manufacturer and shop-owner. He grew up in the Brooklyn area of New York, leaving high school in 1932. This was the period of the Depression in America when economic disaster overtook many ordinary families, including the Millers, as well as causing the ruin of many large businesses and their owners. As his family could not afford the fees for him to go to college, Arthur Miller decided, like many other young Americans, to earn the money himself, so for two years he worked for a salary of fifteen dollars a week in a warehouse that supplied spare parts for automobiles. He later dramatised the experience affectionately in *A Memory of Two Mondays* (1955). In 1934 he entered the University of Michigan to study history and economics, graduating in 1938. It was at college that he began writing plays and won at least three prizes for his work; he also supported himself by working part-time as a journalist.

The Depression was still blighting employment prospects when he left college, and it made a deep impression on him. Not only are the lives of the characters in his plays often affected by it, but it seems certain that it was the experience of those years, when he was forced to earn what he could in all sorts of humbly-paid jobs, that gave him his compassionate understanding of the insecurity of man in modern industrialised urban civilisation and the firm belief in social responsibility that characterises so much of his work. In another way, however, the Depression contributed positively to his career as a dramatist. In order to keep alive an interest in the arts at this time and to create employment for young people like him, the United States Government had set up the Federal Theatre Project during the economic crisis, and by working with that Miller was able to learn much about the craft of the theatre in the company of experts such as Clifford Odets, a leading playwright of the time, as well as the actor Lee J. Cobb, and the director Elia Kazan, both of whom were later to be involved in the production of Miller's best known play, *Death of a Salesman*. The Federal Theatre Project, not surprisingly, encouraged the kind of drama that dealt with the problems of contemporary society, and this coincided conveniently with Miller's own interests and inclinations.

His first play to achieve the distinction of being produced on Broadway, the centre of the American commercial theatre, was called *The Man who Had All the Luck*. It opened in 1944 but failed after only four performances. Meanwhile Miller had begun working as a journalist, had published a book about American soldiers in wartime called *Situation Normal* (also in 1944), and followed this in 1945 with a novel, *Focus*, that dealt vividly with anti-Semitism in New York. Miller's own origins are Jewish but in this novel he chose to write about the problem not from the point of view of a Jew but from that of a Gentile who, because of his appearance, is always mistaken for a Jew. In 1947 he achieved his first success on Broadway with *All My Sons* and followed it in 1949 with the famous *Death of a Salesman*. Both plays are concerned with the strains and pressures of twentieth-century life in the world of American business; both deal critically, though not wholly unsympathetically, with their central characters who are businessmen. For this reason the plays are often thought of as attacks on capitalist society, but this interpretation of them is by no means beyond dispute.

Then, in 1953, came *The Crucible*. At first sight it might seem strange that a dramatist who had made a name for himself with hard-hitting, realistic plays about the America of his own day should now turn to events that had taken place in a very different America almost three hundred years earlier, and stranger still that a man of Jewish extraction should choose to write so knowledgeably and with such insight about Puritans and Puritanism in what might look like a dramatisation of history, powerful and vivid perhaps, but quite remote from our own time.

To understand the reasons for this the situation in America in the 1950s has to be remembered. The Second World War, which had ended in 1945, had established the United States securely, for the first time in its history, as a major world power, and Americans were assuming their new international role with confidence. At the same time the war had left a strong determination that no totalitarian forms of government must ever be allowed to develop as Hitler's National Socialism had developed between the wars, and Russia, although a wartime ally, was being watched very uneasily because of the totalitarian aspects of international Communism. America was fighting a war in Korea to stem the spread of Communism in Asia, and there was an intense, if exaggerated, fear that Communism might even be infiltrating American government and American public life.

Congress reacted to this by setting up the House Un-American Activities Committee, and the Senator for Wisconsin, Joseph R. McCarthy, as chairman of the Senate's Permanent Sub-committee on Investigations, enquired vigorously and unscrupulously into the activities of any person or institution suspected of being in any way sympathetic to Communism. The names of many innocent people were unjustifiably smeared in this unsavoury process and many careers were ruined. Important as the interests of national security were, some people became worried at what was being done in its name: was not a new tyranny developing in their midst with the excuse that it was protecting democracy? The excessive zeal of possibly well-intentioned but certainly fanatical extremists was generating fear and hysteria in a way that began to recall events in Massachusetts in 1692 when a similar situation had precipitated a persecution of people suspected of witchcraft, many of whom had been hanged on the most flimsy evidence before sanity was restored to public life. At least three American dramatists in 1952 and 1953 wrote plays about the Salem witch trials, all of which were oblique comments on the mass hysteria that seemed again to be sweeping America. Of these *The Crucible* is the most celebrated: its first production ran for nearly two hundred performances and it has already achieved the status of a modern classic.

Miller on McCarthyism

In this book the play will be discussed on its own merits as an historical drama, and as a general statement on the effect that fear and fanaticism can have on human beings individually and collectively. The excesses of McCarthyism, as the phenomenon of the 1950s came to be called, seem fortunately to be receding into the past, although there can of course be no guarantee that other circumstances will not in the future produce something similar. It may, however, be helpful to fix *The Crucible* more firmly in the context of the 1950s before moving on.

Interest in the Salem witch trials was not new. Another of the projects undertaken by the government as part of the job-creation programmes of the 1930s had been the collecting together into a three-volume typescript in 1938 of as many original documents as possible relating to the trials and the events that preceded them. Then in 1949 the story had been told again by an historian. In the introduction to her book* she had made it clear that she saw it as 'an allegory of our times'; she referred to the 'ideological intensities which rent their age no less than they do ours', and expressed the hope 'that leaders of the modern world

* Marion L. Starkey in *The Devil in Massachusetts*, Knopf, New York, 1949.

can in the end deal with delusion as sanely and courageously as the men of old Massachusetts dealt with theirs'. This was written before McCarthyism had begun, yet she could comment (no doubt with the atrocities of Nazi Germany in mind) that in Salem 'only twenty witches were executed, a microscopic number compared to . . . the millions who have died in the species of witch-hunt peculiar to our own rational, scientific times'.

Miller's ethnic origins and his liberal political views made him very much aware of this issue in its modern form and as a general question of social morality. In 1950 he had written for the American stage an adaptation of Henrik Ibsen's play *An Enemy of the People* which had first appeared in 1884. It seemed to him topical because, as he said in his introduction, it too posed 'the question of whether the democratic guarantees protecting political minorities ought to be set aside in time of crisis'. McCarthy of course was to argue that the threat from Communism did indeed constitute a crisis in which those who sympathised with Communism could not with safety be allowed the normal democratic rights of free speech. Miller, as a matter of principle, was to oppose this, but that was still in the future. *An Enemy of the People* dealt also with the problem of 'the individual who insists that he is right while the vast majority is absolutely wrong', a situation which, Miller saw, no organised society ever could or ever would tolerate calmly. In stating it in these terms he seemed to be preparing himself for writing *The Crucible*, for in that play circumstances are to put the hero in exactly that position.

When *The Crucible* appeared reviewers referred to it as a parable and it was generally recognised as such. In an interview given in October 1953 to the periodical *Theatre Arts* Miller understandably spoke very guardedly about this aspect of the play, but he did allow himself the generalisation 'When you have an ideology which feels itself so pure, it implies an extreme view of the world. Because they are white, opposition is completely black'. McCarthyism certainly saw the antagonism in those terms, and Miller's next observation, although again a general one, was equally apt: 'We have come to a time when it seems there must be two sides, and we look back to the ideal state of being, when there was no conflict'. Not only does he realise how unachievable that ideal state is, but he recognises that it is undesirable, because it is only out of the conflict of views (not necessarily expressed in violence) that progress comes. He may also have remembered George Bernard Shaw's epigram, 'No conflict, no drama'.

The Crucible dramatises that conflict well, and when in 1957 Miller wrote an introduction to the collected edition of his plays he was able to speak more candidly about the links between that play and McCarthyism, while rightly pointing out that the play deals with themes much larger and less localised than that. Any reader of these notes should certainly study that introduction for the light it throws on Miller's purpose and practice. What particularly worried Miller in the McCarthy years was the readiness with which men handed over their consciences to other men: this too became a prominent theme in the play.

It is sometimes suggested that the parallel between 1692 and the McCarthy years is unreal because the witchcraft which the Puritans feared was purely a delusion, whereas the Communist subversion feared in the 1950s was certainly a fact even though its significance may have been exaggerated. This is to ignore Miller's main point that when, out of fear and fanaticism, men over-react to a situation, be it real or imaginary, they deny their intelligence, their humanity, and their moral autonomy. When mere suspicion itself is accepted as evidence, it matters little whether what is suspected has a basis in fact or not. Ironically, events were soon to show him how uncomfortably near to the truth the play came.

Miller's subsequent career

In 1954 there was a production of *The Crucible* in Brussels to which Miller was naturally invited. He was, however, refused a visa by the State Department on the grounds that he was a supporter of the Communist cause. He denied this, and published a bitterly satiric essay entitled 'A Modest Proposal for Pacification of the Public Temper'. In 1956 he was required to appear before the House Un-American Activities Committee and his impressive refutation of the charges against him led to the conditional restoration of his passport. However, he refused to give the Committee the names of people he had seen at Communist-sponsored meetings of writers that he had attended in the 1940s, and for this, in 1957, he was found guilty of contempt of Congress. No punishment was imposed, and the conviction was reversed a year later, but Miller must often have thought how justified he had been to call attention in *The Crucible* to the abiding need for men to adhere firmly to their principles in the face of oppression. In his later plays, especially in the autobiographical *After the Fall* (1964), he has returned to this moral problem of divided loyalties, but always to insist that a man's first loyalty must be to his beliefs.

Since *The Crucible* Miller has written ten more plays of varying quality, the best among them being *A View from the Bridge* (1957) and *The Price* (1968). He has never again attempted an historical subject, though two later plays are dramatisations of the biblical story of the creation of the world. He has achieved an international reputation as a man of letters, has published a number of short stories, one script for the cinema and two for television, as well as many critical essays on his own works and on those of other people.

Arthur Miller has been married three times. Divorce from his first wife in 1956 enabled him to marry the glamorous film star Marilyn Monroe (for whom *The Misfits* was written) but that too ended in divorce, followed later by her suicide. *After the Fall* is in part concerned with that relationship in a way that many people have found embarrassing in the candour of its revelation. Since 1962 he has been married to an Austrian-born photographer, Ingeborg Morath, on whom another character in *After the Fall* seems to be based. Even if he publishes nothing further, his reputation seems secure as a major American literary figure of the postwar period and a dramatist of distinction.

Until comparatively recent times there has never been in America the vigorous theatrical tradition that has flourished in Britain and Europe since the sixteenth century. Although theatres were established in most large towns during the nineteenth century, New York is still the main centre of dramatic activity. Because the theatre has not had the social and cultural significance that it possesses in Europe, it has attracted few major writers, yet in the past half-century three playwrights in particular have revitalised American drama and given it international significance. Miller is one of them; another is his great predecessor, Eugene O'Neill (1888-1953), who died in the year that *The Crucible* appeared; the third is Miller's contemporary, Tennessee Williams (*b*.1911), whose plays, more torrid and sensational than Miller's, are often contrasted with his so as to suggest that Miller is the more coldly intellectual, Williams the more passionate, writer; this is, however, very much of an over-simplified view of their qualities. Among the works of these three, *The Crucible* as an historical play remains unique, though its preoccupation with ordinary people keeps it firmly in the mainstream of American drama.

A note on the text

The text of the play that is printed in Arthur Miller, *Collected Plays*, Viking Press, New York, 1957; Cresset Press, London 1958 has been used in these *Notes*. Nine months after the play opened, however, a version of the text was published in a periodical (*Theatre Arts*, New York, October, 1953). This text differed from that used in the original production, but in the final month of its run that production was revised to conform to this text. The major change Miller made was the addition of one short new scene at the beginning of what is now Act Three. However, when the volume of his *Collected Plays* was published, he had again changed his mind, and this scene was omitted. It has accordingly been ignored in the summaries of the play in Part 2 of this book, but, because its addition and subsequent omission throw some light on Miller's attitude towards the play and its characters, it is discussed in Part 3. The text of this scene, for those who wish to read it, is reprinted in *Twentieth Century Interpretations of The Crucible*, edited by John H. Ferres, Prentice-Hall, Englewood Cliffs, New Jersey, 1972, pp. 109–112.

The *Collected Plays* text is divided into four acts, but the acting edition, though structurally the same (with the addition of the extra scene), called the present Acts One and Two, Act I Scene 1 and Scene 2; the extra scene and the present Acts Three and Four became Act II, Scenes 1, 2, and 3. The dialogue in *Collected Plays* has in some places been expanded from the earlier text and has been changed in others. Particularly interesting examples of these changes are instanced in Parts 2 and 3, but it has not been felt necessary to identify or list every such change.

Miller himself has contributed a great deal to the critical discussion of this play, and this commentary naturally takes his views into account. They occur principally in three places, and, for convenience, they are referred to hereafter by the short titles listed below:

Introduction: the Introduction to *Collected Plays*, especially pages 38 to 47.

Background Essay: the commentary in Act One that follows the opening stage direction and precedes the beginning of the action (pages 225 to 229 of *Collected Plays*).

Theatre Arts interview: the interview with Miller reproduced in *Theatre Arts*, October, 1953 when the text of the play was printed.

Part 2

Summaries
of THE CRUCIBLE

THIS IS A PLAY and is therefore designed to make its effect on the stage rather than in the study. The summaries are therefore intended to give some impression of its theatrical impact: that is to say, the summaries are based on the dialogue and the action which we would hear and see in the theatre. The stage directions are referred to only when it is essential and the Summaries (and the Notes and Glossaries that follow them) do not make any direct reference to the prose commentary with which Miller, especially in Act One, interrupts the dialogue at times. These and the Introduction will of course be taken into account in the commentary on the play in Part 3. Their presence in the text is an indication of Miller's desire to reach a reading audience as well as playgoers, and they should be studied by the reader of these Notes, but preferably when he is more familiar with the plot and the characters.

A general summary

In this play, by a skilful interweaving of fact and fiction, Miller creates an impression of the panic that struck the little town of Salem, Massachusetts, in 1692 when the inhabitants feared that there had been an outbreak of witchcraft in their midst and the authorities took drastic measures to locate it and stamp it out. It shows that superstition and fear, feeding on petty rivalries and mistrust among ordinary people, can become fanaticism and cruelty, disrupting an entire community.

Witchcraft is suspected when two young girls fall mysteriously ill after having taken part in some childish magic rites with a black slave in the woods at night. The father of one child is Samuel Parris, the minister of the town; the father of the other is a wealthy landowner, known to be greedy for more land. Both men have enemies in the town, so that not everyone is prepared to believe their charges of witchcraft. In particular, a local farmer, John Proctor, is outspokenly sceptical. However, another clergyman, the Reverend Hale, is brought to the town and he secures from the black slave a 'confession' that she has conjured up the Devil.

The girls are now credited with the power to identify witches; all whom they denounce, on whatever grounds, are arrested and brought to trial. This includes elderly women who have always led blameless lives, as well as Proctor's wife Elizabeth. The girls' ringleader is the minister's niece, Abigail, with whom Proctor has had illicit sexual relations. He suspects that she has denounced Elizabeth so that she may herself marry him if Elizabeth is hanged, but he cannot convince other people of this. This is partly because he has never made any secret of his dislike of Parris, and is thus suspected of wishing to overthrow authority; partly because the girls are venerated so foolishly that no one will hear anything said against them. Proctor persuades one of them to admit publicly that the witchcraft was all make-believe, but she is so intimidated by the others and by the authorities that she withdraws what she has said and it is Proctor who is arrested.

Meanwhile other innocent people have been condemned and the fanatical zeal of the authorities has terrified more into silence. The Reverend Hale, suspecting the truth, has begun to regret his involvement in the proceedings but believes that the best way of atoning for this is to persuade the condemned people to save their lives by 'confessing' their guilt in order to be pardoned. Proctor is tempted by this suggestion but at the last minute recognises how dishonest it is and goes to his death rather than lie.

Although the play ends with his death, there is a strong suggestion that his example will strengthen the resistance of others, that some at least of the authorities realise how misled they have been by Abigail (who has now fled the country with one of the other girls), and that sanity and peace may return to Salem.

Detailed summaries

Act One

The Reverend Samuel Parris, minister of religion in Salem, Massachusetts, is praying at the bedside of his ten-year-old daughter Betty, who is unconscious. His West Indian slave Tituba is obviously worried about the girl but he orders her out of the room. His niece, Abigail Williams, brings in another girl who tells him that the doctor can find in his books no cure for Betty's illness and suspects that the cause might be unnatural. Parris denies this possibility and sends her home, but Abigail tells him that the rumours of witchcraft are widespread in Salem. This alarms Parris, not only because of his daughter's illness but because he knows he has enemies who would be glad to see him driven out of his ministry and he fears that this may give them an excuse for action against him.

On the previous night he has found Abigail, Betty, and their friends dancing in the woods; at least one of them was naked and Tituba was swaying and making strange noises. Fearing that they were engaged in some practice of witchcraft which has caused Betty's illness, he urges Abigail to tell him the whole truth about the episode but the girl insists that it was only a harmless game, and that her own reputation is spotless even though no one will employ her since she was dismissed from the service of Mrs Proctor.

They are joined by Thomas Putnam and his wife whose daughter Ruth is in the same condition as Betty and who are very ready to attribute it to witchcraft. Seven of Mrs Putnam's children have died within a few hours of their birth and, believing Tituba to have magic powers, she sent Ruth to her in the woods on the previous evening to find out the reason. Parris now has his suspicions confirmed: witchcraft was being practised though Abigail still protests her innocence. Putnam urges him to declare this publicly but Parris will not agree to do so yet. He leaves with the Putnams to reassure the townspeople when the Putnams' servant, Mercy Lewis, has brought them news of a slight improvement in Ruth.

Left alone, Abigail and Mercy discuss how much of their activities of the previous night they ought to admit to, now that some aspects of it are known. Another girl, Mary Warren, arrives to tell them that the rumour of witchcraft is spreading; thoroughly frightened, she advises them to tell the truth. At this moment Betty suddenly recovers consciousness. Hysterically she rushes to the window saying that she wishes to fly to her dead mother, but the others restrain her. Betty accuses Abigail of having drunk blood as a means of causing the death of her former employer, Mrs Proctor, but Abigail silences her by hitting her and threatening the other girls with violence unless they too say nothing of the night's events.

John Proctor enters in search of Mary Warren who has succeeded Abigail as their servant; he orders her home and Mercy leaves when Mary does. Alone with her former employer, Abigail assures him that it was only girlish fun, not witchcraft, in the woods. It quickly becomes clear from her conversation that their relationship has been more than that of master and servant. Proctor teases her at first but, realizing that she is again trying to make herself sexually attractive to him, he tells her firmly that their previous intimacy must not be resumed. Claiming that he still loves her, Abigail tries to embrace him, blaming his wife for his changed attitude. A quarrel between them is averted as Betty sits up screaming and her father rushes in, followed by the Putnams and Mercy Lewis, whom he sends to fetch the doctor.

Two more townspeople now arrive, Rebecca Nurse and Giles Corey.

Both are elderly, and Rebecca's presence not only quietens Betty but seems also to reassure the adults by her gentleness and common sense. She advises them against assuming too quickly that witchcraft is involved, though she cannot explain the deaths of the Putnam babies. Parris has already said that he has sent for another minister, the Reverend Hale, who is an authority on witchcraft. Proctor argues that Parris should not have done this without the approval of the senior members of the church. Rebecca thinks that they should trust in medicine and prayer. Putnam's support of Parris brings a quarrel with Proctor who does not like the severity of the minister's sermons. The antagonisms in the town are now becoming apparent. Parris begins an argument, which in these circumstances must sound very trivial, as to whether his contract requires the townspeople to provide him with wood for his fire without payment; he exaggerates their dislike for him into a threat to the church and to God. His enemies, he claims, are organised into a group against him. Proctor angrily declares his intention of finding this group and joining it, though it is clear that he does not really believe in its existence at all. Rebecca tries to reconcile the two men but Corey's support for the minister leads to another quarrel over property rights, this time between Putnam and Proctor. In this, Corey swings back to the support of Proctor, but the quarrel is cut short by the arrival of the Reverened Hale.

He is introduced to the townspeople and greets them courteously. Proctor leaves, after bluntly expressing his belief that what is needed in Salem is common sense, and Hale begins his investigations. He is a learned and serious man but, in Rebecca's view, too inclined to listen to the superstitious fears of people like Putnam, and so she leaves them in her quietly dignified way. Corey claims that his wife's reading of a book makes it impossible for him to pray and asks Hale to explain this, but Hale is more anxious to enquire into Betty's condition. Parris, who clearly believes that the Devil is at work in Salem, is still puzzled as to why his household has been chosen but both he and Corey accept Hale's explanation that the Devil will gain greater respect for himself by entering the home of a good man than that of a sinner.

Hale cross-examines Abigail on the events in the wood. Characteristically anxious to deny her own involvement in them, she blames Tituba for everything that has happened. The slave is brought in and is terrified by the accusations Abigail brings against her but her frightened attempts at denial only convince the men that she is guilty. Parris and Putnam threaten her violently, but Hale tries to secure a confession by assuring her of God's love for her. The rapidity with which questions are now put to her perplexes the ignorant and frightened woman even more. Realising that her own safety depends upon giving them the information they want, she begins to describe her dealings with the Devil and to name the townspeople she has seen in his company.

There is no reason for us to accept this as anything more than the hysterical reaction of a simple woman in hostile surroundings and in fear of her life; instinctively she seizes on this line of action as in her own best interest. The others, of course, are very willing to believe her, especially when Abigail joins in the 'confession'. She too names people she has seen with the Devil, and Betty does the same. Hale and Parris are, of course, instantly convinced that Betty is cured and the act ends with the alternating cries of the two girls denouncing more people in their mounting frenzy.

NOTES AND GLOSSARY
Like the opening act of any play, this act has as part of its function what is known as exposition—that is, giving the audience enough information about what has happened before the action of the play begins so as to enable them to understand what is happening now. At the same time it has to set the action of the play in motion, to engage the audience's interest in it, and to sustain their curiosity as to the eventual outcome of the play. The reader might usefully, at this point, pause and consider for himself in what ways and with what success each of these four objectives has been achieved. Imagining himself in the theatre as the curtain falls on the first act, he should ask himself these questions: what sort of a community does Salem seem to be, and how well do the inhabitants get on with one another? Has anything encouraged me to be more sympathetic to some characters than to others and if so, to which, and why? How sure can I be that I know exactly what took place in the wood, and in what ways, if any, has the play made me curious to know more about it? What direction does the action of the play now seem likely to take, and is this the direction that I would like to see it take? Which moments of this act were particularly exciting to watch, and why?

Some comments are needed on the language of the play as a whole, as well as on individual words and phrases in this act. The vocabulary is simple, most words being used in their normal dictionary meaning. However, to keep us aware that these are simple country people of a period different from our own, Miller allows them occasional peculiarities of expression. This is not to be thought of as an exact rendering of the way in which English was spoken in seventeenth-century Massachusetts but rather as an attempt to give an archaic flavour to the language so as to distance the play from the twentieth century. The costumes the characters wear have this effect also, of course, but the language adds something to the solemnity of the play as well.

Many of these devices the reader has met in this act and he will quickly become familiar with them. The most obvious is the substitution of one form of the verb for another: 'it were' instead of 'it was', 'it be' instead of 'it is', 'she give' instead of 'she gave', and so on. Another is the use of 'Let you ...' to give emphasis to a verb: 'Let you take hold here', says Putnam to Parris, meaning 'Take firm control of this situation!'. In a slightly different sense it can mean 'if', as when Abigail threatens the girls: 'Let either of you breathe a word ... and I will bring a pointy reckoning [a sharp punishment]'. Sometimes the modern use of the auxiliary 'do' is omitted: Proctor says 'I like not ...' where today he would say 'I do not like ...' and 'What say you ...?' instead of 'What do you say ...?' 'Pray you ...' is often used where we would say 'Please ...' Married women are addressed as 'Goody ...' rather than 'Mrs ...'; this seventeenth-century usage was an abridgement of the term 'Goodwife ...'

These phrases are used by all the people; in addition, of course, Tituba, a black West Indian slave, speaks English less accurately than the other characters, but except in the instances glossed below her meaning is usually clear enough.

Other idioms occurring in Act One have the following meanings:

hearty *(used by Tituba):* healthy
I cannot blink what I saw *(Parris):* I cannot ignore [shut my eyes to] what I saw
I'll show you a great doin' on your arse one of these days *(Proctor):* half-humorously echoing Mary's phrase, Proctor is threatening to chastise her for disobedience. 'Arse' is a colloquial term for the buttocks.
I'd admire to know ... *(Corey):* I'd like very much to know ...

Some of the words and phrases used have a particular meaning associated with seventeenth-century Puritan religious belief; the most important are these (listed in the order in which they occur in Act One):

open with me ... *(Parris);* **open yourself ...** *(Hale):* confess solemnly to me the whole truth ...
these stiff-necked people *(Parris):* these stubborn people (a biblical phrase)
it is a providence *(Putnam):* It is a very fortunate thing (with the added implication that it is divinely ordained)

. . . these Christian women and their covenanted men *(Abigail):* full membership of the Puritan church was reserved for those who had entered into a covenant (a solemn and binding undertaking) to accept its discipline. It suggests also that the men are covenanted to the women in marriage

mark it for a sign *(Mrs Putnam):* Take note of this as special evidence of God's grace

This society *(Proctor);* **the society** *(Rebecca):* not merely the people of Salem in general but specifically the covenanted members of the church

We are not Quakers *(Parris):* the Quakers were another Christian sect of whom the Puritans disapproved strongly because the Quakers believed that God could inspire ordinary people to communicate His message to others, whereas the Puritans taught that God communicated only through ordained ministers. When Proctor says 'I may speak my heart, I think', he means only that he has the right to say what he believes, but Parris sees it as a deliberate threat to his authority as a minister and accuses Proctor of adopting Quaker practices.

I go to God for you *(Rebecca):* I pray that God will guide you

Other phrases relate to the belief in witchcraft, and the use of the word 'spirit' in particular needs explanation. The rites in which the girls have engaged in the wood are described as 'conjuring spirits': that is to say, summoning by magic means the spirits of the dead back to earth, or summoning supernatural beings evilly disposed to humans, as, in particular, the Devil. Elsewhere in this Act these are referred to as 'loose spirits' and the process is called 'trafficking with spirits', 'trucking with the Devil', and 'compacting with the Devil' (though the last phrase has the added meaning of signing an agreement with the Devil). Hale lists the various forms and disguises believed to be adopted by 'familiar spirits'; 'familiar' here does not mean simply 'well-known' but implies that the spirit is at the service of one particular human being. When that human being wishes to harm another by invisible, supernatural means he or she is said to 'send his spirit out against' that person. The Devil (also referred to by Hale as 'Satan' and 'the Old Boy') was believed to have a forked tail and a cloven (divided) hoof: hence Mrs Putnam's reference to death driving into the children 'forked and hoofed'.

Witches were believed to have sold their souls to the Devil in return for the power to harm others by these means. Their victims were said to be possessed by spirits who could be driven out only by a minister of God. Hale, hoping to cure Betty, uses a Latin phrase from the ritual of exorcism: translated it means 'In the name of the Christian God and His Son, go out from this girl and return to Hell'.

Act Two

The scene is now the living-room of John Proctor's farmhouse outside the town and eight days have elapsed. John comes in at the end of a day's farming. He tastes the meal his wife Elizabeth has prepared for him, adds more salt, and is washing when Elizabeth enters. It is a familiar domestic evening scene with the wife asking the husband about his day's work and the husband complimenting the wife on the meal. Proctor comments particularly on how well the food is seasoned but does not mention that he has put in more salt. He obviously wishes his wife to take the credit for this and she, unknowingly, is happy to do so. His conversation about the farm, the weather, his plans to buy a young cow for her, and the beauty of the spring, is gentle and affectionate: it is almost unnecessary for him to tell her of his desire to please her, yet from her replies, which are short and non-committal, as well as from her failure to return his kiss, we realise that all is not well between them.

Proctor remarks on her sadness and she tells him the news from Salem. Despite his orders, she has been unable to prevent Mary Warren from going to the town that day: Mary has been made an official of the court that has been set up under the Deputy Governor of Massachusetts to investigate the outbreak of witchcraft. Elizabeth tells Proctor that Abigail and the other girls, when confronted with people suspected of witchcraft, scream and fall to the floor. The people are then convicted of bewitching them: fourteen have already been imprisoned and are likely to be hanged if they do not confess. Proctor is contemptuous of these proceedings, and Elizabeth urges him to go to Salem and tell the court the truth. Although neither of them can at first bear to name Abigail, it is what she has told Proctor in Parris's house that Elizabeth wishes him to disclose: that it had only been play in the woods, not witchcraft. Proctor tells his wife that he may not be believed because he and Abigail had been alone and without witnesses when she told him. His wife had not known this, and her changed attitude shows that suspicions she had formerly had of her husband have been reawakened. Were it not Abigail that he had to accuse, she tells him, he would not hesitate. His rather blustering reaction to this is to accuse Elizabeth of being cold and unforgiving in her desire to judge him. His aggressively self-defensive tone contrasts with her calmer answers and suggests that she has some justification for her suspicions.

A quarrel is averted by the return of Mary Warren who, when Proctor scolds her for her disobedience, complains of feeling unwell. She gives Elizabeth a doll she has made for her during the day and seems unusually docile in her manner. Questioned, she admits that the number of accused women has now risen to thirty-nine, and that one of them is to be hanged. Mary also tells them that another, Sarah Good, has confessed to bewitching people, thus confirming Mary's own suspicions of her. The grounds for these suspicions are chiefly that, when asking for charity, the old woman had muttered to herself; in court she had claimed to be repeating the Ten Commandments, but when required to say them aloud could not remember any one of them. Proctor forbids Mary to return to the court but she replies that she must continue doing God's work, adding, as evidence of a miracle, that Sarah Good has been found to be pregnant despite her age. Still contemptuous, Proctor threatens to whip her, only to be told that she has saved Elizabeth's life.

Husband and wife are both stunned at this news. Mary will not name Elizabeth's accuser and, trying to preserve her dignity, retires to bed. Elizabeth clearly suspects that her enemy is Abigail who is jealous of her and would like to see her dead. Elizabeth urges her husband to see Abigail and break off his relationship with her finally. Proctor agrees to do so, but with such reluctance and self-righteousness that his wife's suspicions increase.

Suddenly they become aware of the arrival of the Reverend Hale. Less sure of himself than he was in Act One, he tells them that both Elizabeth and Rebecca Nurse have been mentioned in court, though not formally accused. Both Proctors are appalled that Rebecca is suspected, but Hale tells them that the possibility of her guilt cannot be entirely eliminated. He then proceeds to question Proctor about his irregular church attendance. After some excuses about his wife's illness, Proctor admits his dislike of the Reverend Parris who, he believes, is more interested in the wealth of the church than in his religion. For this reason he has not allowed Parris to baptise the youngest Proctor boy. Hale cannot approve of this but is relieved to know that Proctor has helped with the building of the church. Elizabeth assures him that they are both devout Christians and that she knows the Commandments. When Proctor is asked to repeat them, however, he forgets one: significantly, it is the one that forbids adultery. His wife prompts him and, smiling, he claims that between them they know all ten.

Hale cannot take this so lightly and Elizabeth realises that he still suspects her. She urges her husband to tell him what he knows of the whole affair, but when Proctor does so, and quotes Abigail as the source of his information, Hale rejects it because others have confessed to dealing with the Devil that night. Proctor asks whether Hale has never suspected that, faced with death, people will confess to anything. Hale admits that he has thought of that, but a stage direction tells us that he does not wish to believe it. Quickly changing the subject, he asks Proctor whether he will testify in court against Abigail. Proctor tells him that he will, though he fears that people who will suspect so honest a woman as his wife are unlikely to believe him.

Changing the subject again, Hale asks whether it is true that Proctor does not believe in witches. Uncertain how best to answer, Proctor takes refuge in suggesting that, as the Bible refers to witches, it is not for him to deny them. Elizabeth is asked the same question and, with her characteristic uncompromising honesty, says that she does not believe in them. Hale is scandalised and suggests that she is rejecting the Bible. The vigour with which Proctor denies this and the quiet confidence with which Elizabeth asserts her innocence seem to convince Hale, and he urges them to resume church attendance and have the child baptised.

As we begin to think that the Proctors will be safe after all, Giles Corey arrives with the news that both his wife and Rebecca Nurse have now been arrested. Rebecca's husband Francis enters and tells them that she is charged with the murder of the Putnam babies. To him this seems so unrealistic as to be ridiculous, but Hale sees it only as possible evidence of the extent to which Salem is in the grip of evil powers. Nevertheless he promises Nurse that his wife will have a fair trial, though the fact that she is to be tried at all is a shock to Nurse, as it is to Proctor who is angered at any suggestion of her guilt. Corey then says that his wife has been charged with killing by witchcraft a pig that she had sold to a neighbour. Corey seems to realise that his own complaint about his wife's reading may have led to the neighbour making this accusation.

Before they can discuss this any further, however, Ezekiel Cheever, an officer of the court, arrives with the town marshal bringing a warrant for Elizabeth's arrest, one of sixteen warrants issued in the short time since Hale left Salem for the Proctors' farm. Abigail has accused Elizabeth, and Cheever has been told to search for any dolls in the house. Elizabeth denies having any, forgetting the one that Mary Warren has given her, but Cheever sees this and takes it, commanding Elizabeth to accompany him. Proctor, however, tells her to fetch Mary, and while she is gone Cheever inspects the doll. Lifting its skirt, he finds a needle stuck into its body. Amazed, he describes how Abigail, taken ill at dinner, was found to have a needle stuck in her stomach. She had blamed Elizabeth for this and Cheever believes the needle in the doll to be Elizabeth's method of harming Abigail by witchcraft. Proctor points out that Abigail must have stuck both needles in herself, but Cheever is convinced and Hale remains silent.

Mary is brought in and questioned; frightened and confused, she admits that she may herself have left the needle in the doll. Proctor expects Hale to accept this explanation, but Elizabeth demands to know why there is so much fuss about a needle. When she is told, her indignation at Abigail leads her to exclaim that the girl should be put to death. This seems even further proof of guilt to Cheever who tries to remove Elizabeth, but Proctor in his anger tears up the warrant, to the horror of the officials, and he orders them out of his house. Hale repeats his assurance that, if Elizabeth is innocent, the court will be just. Proctor is even angrier that his wife's innocence should be doubted at all and he asks one of the play's key questions: 'Is the accuser always holy now?'. He is also infuriated by Hale's neutrality.

Elizabeth, realistic as ever, recognises that she will have to go with the officials. Briefly she gives Mary housekeeping instructions and tells Proctor not to frighten their children with talk of witchcraft. She leaves with dignity, but when the sound of chains is heard outside Proctor rushes out to stop them chaining her and returns swearing vengeance on the marshal. Mary is in tears; Hale is distressed but, to Corey's disgust, still takes no action. He promises Proctor to say what he can in Elizabeth's favour but it is plain that he believes Salem has in some way drawn down upon itself the judgement of God for some offence committed in the past. He leaves, exhorting the townspeople to reflect on this, and Proctor, who has just called Hale a coward, is troubled by Hale's obvious sincerity. Corey departs, planning with Proctor to meet again in the morning. Nurse presumably leaves with him, although there is no stage direction to say so, and Proctor is left alone with Mary.

He tells her that she must accompany him to the court the next day and declare the whole truth, but she is frightened of Abigail and warns Proctor that Abigail will denounce him for having had sexual relations with her. Once he knows that Abigail has told Mary of this, he is even more determined to save Elizabeth by exposing Abigail. The scene ends with Mary protesting that she cannot do this, while Proctor threatens and shakes her violently, realising that no other choice is now open to him than to reveal his own guilt publicly to save his wife.

NOTES AND GLOSSARY

Looking back on this act, the reader should try to identify for himself the moments of greatest tension, the ways in which his impressions of the individual characters have been changed by what has happened in this act, and the means by which Miller has tried to keep alive the audience's interest in the developing plot.

Again, a few phrases need explanation:

It's a fair poppet *(Elizabeth):* It's a pretty doll (compare the modern word 'puppet')

I'll official you! *(Proctor):* again, as in Act One, Proctor echoes Mary's phrase mockingly as he threatens to whip her. His meaning is that, by punishing her as a disobedient servant, he will show her how little her newfound officialdom really means

She will cry me out *(Elizabeth):* Abigail will denounce me

Why do you anger with me? *(Elizabeth):* Why do you become angry at me?

She has an arrow in you yet *(Elizabeth):* Abigail still has a hold on your affections. (The classical god of love was said to make people fall in love by shooting at them with his arrows)

It rebels my stomach *(Hale):* My stomach rebels against it

. . . naught to do with witchcraft *(Proctor):* . . . nothing to do with witchcraft

You surely do not fly against the Gospel *(Hale):* You surely do not contradict the word of God (and see 'Gospel' below)

Again, many phrases relate to Christian doctrine:

The crowd will part like the sea for Israel *(Elizabeth):* In the Bible (Exodus 14) when Moses led the Israelites out of captivity in Egypt, God is said to have divided the waters of the Red Sea to allow them to cross in safety. The simile indicates the respect given to Abigail and her friends as the agents of God

Learn charity, woman *(Proctor):* in biblical usage 'charity' means 'loving kindness and generosity of spirit'. Proctor uses it in this sense, not in the modern sense of alms-giving

The Ten Commandments, the Commandments *(Mary, Hale, and others):* the ten moral laws governing Jewish and Christian behaviour, delivered by Moses from God to the Israelites, which Christians are expected to know by heart.

The man dreams cathedrals, not clapboard meetin' houses *(Proctor):* the Puritans believed that the elaborate buildings in which other Christian sects worshipped ('cathedrals') and the costly ornaments they used ('golden candlesticks') were an offence to God. Their own churches were simple timber buildings painted white and furnished very sparsely, known as meeting houses. Proctor implies that Parris really hankers after non-Puritan, ostentatious forms of worship, just as, in Act One, Parris had conversely accused him of deviating from Puritanism in the opposite direction, towards Quakerism

The Gospel *(Hale, Proctor, Elizabeth):* the word of God embodied in the Bible, especially the New Testament

Before the Devil fell, God thought him beautiful in Heaven *(Hale):* a reference to the Christian belief that the Devil was an angel whose disobedience caused God to throw him from Heaven into the underworld. (*Paradise Lost* by John Milton (1608–1674) is the best known literary treatment of this.) When Proctor says to Mary later in this Act 'We will slide together into our own pit' he implies that, because of their wickedness, they too will fall to Hell (often called 'the pit') but more gradually than Satan did

Pontius Pilate! *(Proctor):* Proctor is here identifying Hale with the Roman governor before whom Jesus Christ was brought and who, refusing either to condemn or to release Christ, washed his hands to symbolise his refusal to accept responsibility for what was to happen to Christ

---

Act Three

It is the following day and the scene is an empty room outside the courtroom in which the trial of Martha Corey is being conducted. We hear the voice of Judge Hathorne sternly asking why she is a witch and why she persecutes the girls, and Martha's voice denying both. Then her husband's voice is heard demanding that attention be paid to his evidence concerning Thomas Putnam. Because he will not be silent Corey is ejected from the courtroom into the room before us, and the Reverend Hale follows, hoping to pacify him. They are immediately joined by Judge Hathorne and Danforth, the Deputy Governor of

Massachusetts, who is presiding over the court. Parris and Cheever accompany them. Asked why he is noisily interrupting the court's proceedings, Corey answers boldly that he is a man of property in Salem, it is his wife that is on trial, and lies are being told about her. He breaks into tears as he explains that, with no disrespect to the court, he has evidence he wishes to give: he had not intended his remarks about his wife's fondness for books to mean that she was a witch, and he is distressed at the harm he has unintentionally done her. Hale urges that he be heard, but Danforth insists that it must be done formally and in accordance with court procedures.

Francis Nurse speaks next (although the text does not indicate when he has entered). He claims to have evidence that the court is being deceived by Abigail and her friends, and again Danforth asks that this be formally submitted in writing. Hathorne constantly interrupts Danforth in this scene, asking for sterner measures, but Danforth tries not to be influenced by him. Corey brings in Proctor and Mary Warren, much to the alarm of the Reverend Parris, who tries to persuade Danforth not to listen to them. Mary, supported by Proctor, tells them that, despite her previous evidence, she never in fact saw anything supernatural. Parris continues to argue that Proctor and Mary are seeking only to overturn the court and its authority, but Danforth tries to ignore this while he assesses this new and unexpected development.

He cross-examines Proctor vigorously, but Proctor insists that his purpose is only to bring out the truth and save his wife. Cheever, however, reports that Proctor tore up the warrant when his wife was arrested, and Parris complains of the irregularity of his attendance at church and of his ploughing on Sundays. Proctor admits his dislike of Parris but insists that he himself lives according to his Christian beliefs. When Danforth speaks of believing the evidence the girls have shown him, Proctor bluntly asks him why he does not also believe the evidence that women like Rebecca Nurse have given him for years by living godly lives.

After a whispered conversation with Hathorne to confirm his own memory, Danforth now tells Proctor that Elizabeth claims to be pregnant. They have suspected her of inventing this to save herself from execution, but Proctor maintains that she would never lie even in those circumstances. Danforth promises that if indeed she is pregnant her life will be spared for a year: if Proctor's only wish is to save her life, that has now been achieved, and so Danforth asks him to withdraw his statement that the girls have been lying. This Proctor refuses to do, knowing that Rebecca and Martha will still be condemned if he does; but Parris of course sees in his refusal a desire to overthrow authority.

Danforth, however, decides to suspend the other activities of the court in order to hear Proctor's evidence; he is impressed both by Proctor's conduct and by the town marshal's assurance that Proctor is a good man. Proctor first produces a document signed by ninety-one people who testify that they have known Elizabeth, Rebecca, and Martha for many years and have seen no evidence whatever of any evil behaviour on their part. Parris demands that the ninety-one be brought before the court for questioning, and when Nurse objects that he had promised the signatories that no harm should come to them, Parris argues that this is another attack on the court. Even Hale is outraged by this and asks whether every attempt at a defence is to be rejected on those grounds, but Hathorne supports Parris, and Danforth orders that all ninety-one be arrested for questioning. Nurse is understandably distressed at this despite Danforth's assurance that, if they are good Christians, they have nothing to fear. Worried at the way things are going, Danforth now declares that people who are not seen to support the court positively must be assumed to be hostile to it: there is no possibility of compromise. Mary Warren bursts into tears again, causing Danforth to remark that she is obviously unwell, but Proctor whispers words of encouragement to her.

Next he submits Corey's written statement, on the professional quality of which Danforth congratulates Corey. This brings out the fact that Corey has brought thirty-three legal complaints against other people to the courts in the past. He is about to begin on what would doubtless be a long-winded description of one such case tried by Danforth's father when Thomas Putnam is brought in to answer Corey's charge against him. Danforth tells Putnam that he is accused of encouraging his daughter to bring a charge of witchcraft against another landowner, George Jacobs. Putnam of course denies this but Corey, losing his temper, argues that if Jacobs was executed for witchcraft his land would be taken away as part of his punishment, and only Putnam would have enough money to buy so large a property. Moreover, Corey claims that another man heard Putnam say that his daughter, by condemning Jacobs, had given her father a valuable piece of land. As this is only hearsay, Hathorne demands the name of Corey's informant, but Corey, understandably, will not give it: believing himself responsible for his wife's plight and knowing what is to happen to the other ninety-one witnesses, he will not add to his own burden of guilt. Danforth therefore charges Corey with contempt of court. Proctor and Hale try to support Corey's silence, but Hathorne and Parris loudly denounce it and Danforth repeats his statement that innocent people need have no fear of the court. Corey in his fury tries to attack Putnam,

Proctor restrains him, Corey angers Danforth further by accusing the Deputy Governor of wishing to hang them all, and Mary bursts into tears again.

Comforting her, Proctor now produces her sworn statement in which she retracts her former evidence of having seen the Devil and other evil spirits harming people and charges her friends with lying. Impressed by this, Hale tries to stop these proceedings until a lawyer can be appointed to present the case, as Proctor is not qualified to present it in proper legal form. Hale's conscience is troubled by the number of people he has condemned and especially by having that morning signed Rebecca Nurse's death warrant. Danforth's reply is that Hale is emotionally upset by this only because he is not, like Danforth, a trained and experienced lawyer used to such decisions. He argues that, because witchcraft is invisible, the only possible witnesses to it are the witch (who is hardly likely to testify against herself) or her victim. It is therefore on the victim's evidence alone that a court can rely. Hale reminds him that it is precisely the reliability of the victim's evidence that is now in doubt, but Danforth answers that this is for him as a lawyer to determine, and his authority is not to be questioned.

Silently Danforth, Hathorne, and Parris read Mary's statement. Danforth asserts his control of the situation by angrily silencing another attempted interruption by Parris and sends Cheever to fetch the other girls while Danforth questions Mary. He asks her whether Proctor has used any threats to force this confession from her, and he notices that, although she says Proctor did not, her answers are hesitant. He therefore tells her sternly that, if she is telling the truth now, she is admitting that she was lying before and must in either case expect to be imprisoned for it. Weeping, Mary insists that she is no longer lying and has made her peace with God. Cheever brings in Abigail and the only other three girls he can find. Danforth solemnly warns them that Mary has accused them of lying and that if they now confess to this their punishment will be less severe. He also tells them that Mary's evidence may be false, and may be another trick by the Devil to cause confusion: if it is, she will be put to death. Abigail maintains that Mary is lying, despite Danforth's warning that, before he believes this, he will strictly cross-examine Abigail and her friends.

He begins by returning to the question of Elizabeth's doll and Mary's statement that she had herself stuck the needle in it. Abigail denies this, saying that Elizabeth kept other dolls as well. Proctor says that she did not, and when Cheever tells Danforth that Elizabeth admits having had dolls as a girl, her husband reminds the judges that that was long ago, and that Mary has sworn that she saw no dolls in the house. Parris's suggestion that there may have been dolls hidden in the house produces an angry and contemptuous reply from Proctor, but Parris insists that it is with the unseen that they are concerned.

Proctor asks Danforth what possible advantage there is to Mary in thus changing her evidence, unless it be the truth that she is now telling. In that case, Danforth retorts, Proctor is accusing Abigail of attempted murder, and Proctor candidly agrees that he is doing exactly that. He tells the incredulous Danforth of Abigail's irreverent behaviour in church, but Parris finds an excuse for that and Hathorne points out that laughing in church is no proof of intent to murder. Proctor then questions Mary about their dancing in the woods, where Abigail had taken them and where Parris had seen them dancing naked. Parris, who has already tried to stop this line of enquiry by claiming that it is only another attempt to discredit him, now tries to reject Proctor's statement; he is, however, forced by Hale to admit to having told him of seeing the girls dancing, but he will not agree that any were naked.

Hathorne, Danforth, and Parris all challenge Mary's new evidence in the light of her earlier behaviour in the presence of the alleged witches. When Proctor repeats that her fainting was only pretended, they demand that she pretend to faint now. Mary, thoroughly frightened and distressed, says that she cannot do this to order. Proctor is alarmed but the others are triumphant and fire questions rapidly at her, hoping that she will change her evidence again and admit the existence of the evil spirits. From Mary's statements we can understand that her earlier fainting had been induced by a kind of self-hypnosis, but naturally she cannot explain this and her accusers, being unfamiliar with such theories, cannot understand her meaning. Hathorne in particular asks how she could imagine seeing something unless it was actually present, but Danforth, who seems able at least to conceive the possibility of it, again solemnly asks Abigail for the truth. Abigail's first reaction is indignation that her word should be challenged at all (this is, of course, the way in which she has seen Danforth react to Hale and others).

Suddenly she says that she can feel a cold wind blowing through the room and Hathorne confirms that her hand is indeed cold. Taking their cue from her, the other girls at once blame Mary for causing their coldness, and Mary, terrified, breaks down. Proctor, protesting that it is all pretence, attacks Abigail and angrily calls her a whore. When Danforth objects to this, Proctor realises that he has betrayed himself but must now bring out the whole truth. To the distress of his friend Francis Nurse and to the confusion of Danforth, he admits that he and Abigail had had sexual relations in his barn and that this is why Elizabeth dismissed Abigail. It is vengeance, he argues, that Abigail seeks, believing that Elizabeth's death would force Proctor to honour his earlier commitment to Abigail by marriage. Invited to deny this, Abigail again tries to bluff her way out of the difficulty, but Danforth has seen a way of resolving this and is unmoved by her threats.

He questions Proctor, who again asserts his faith in Elizabeth's unfailing truthfulness and who repeats his statement that her dismissal of Abigail was occasioned by her knowledge of his misconduct with the girl. Threatening Abigail with dire punishment if this is proved, Danforth makes her and Proctor turn their backs and remain silent while Elizabeth is brought in and questioned. Asked to say why she dismissed Abigail, Elizabeth is understandably reluctant to shame her husband in public, not knowing that he has already confessed. She therefore compromises by saying that she herself had been ill and had feared that Proctor might have been attracted to the younger woman, but when asked categorically whether Proctor has committed adultery with Abigail she denies it. She then learns with dismay that her husband has already confessed to it and that her lie has served no purpose.

Proctor is, of course, trapped either way. Had Elizabeth told the truth he would have been convicted of adultery, but as he has himself insisted that his wife never lies it appears that he himself must have lied to destroy Abigail and save his wife. Hale is the first to recognise the true situation and to come to Proctor's defence, but before he can complete his denunciation of Abigail she pretends to see a bird threatening to tear her face with its claws, and again the other girls take up the cry. In vain does Proctor point out that there is no bird. They pretend that the bird is Mary in a changed shape, and when Mary addresses them they pretend that they can no longer see her standing in front of them. When Mary assures Danforth that Abigail cannot see any bird the girls repeat her words as though bewitched. The more desperately she appeals to them, the more they mimic her, until Danforth begins to believe that Mary really is controlling them. He exhorts her to admit her complicity with the Devil, while Proctor and Hale urge her to tell the truth, and the girls build up their hysterical performance to a terrifying climax. Understandably all this is too much for the unfortunate Mary who also begins to scream hysterically. As she does so, the others stop and she is left screaming alone.

By now she is beyond Proctor's influence: all she wants is to save herself from this frightening isolation. She denounces him as being in league with the Devil and hysterically invents a detailed account of how he forced her to help him overthrow the court. Unable to stand alone against Abigail and her friends, she submissively rejoins them. Danforth is convinced of Proctor's guilt and ignores Hale's warning that Mary is mentally disturbed. Proctor, too, is overwhelmed by the turn that events have taken. God, he proclaims, is dead, betrayed by men like himself and Danforth who have been afraid of the truth when they saw it and who will be damned for their refusal to declare it. The act ends with the imprisonment of Proctor and Corey, but with the Reverend Hale, his eyes at last opened to the truth, denouncing the court and refusing to take any further part in its activities.

NOTES AND GLOSSARY

At the end of Act Two there was some hope that the action might end happily for the Proctors: by the end of Act Three that seems impossible. What characters, what circumstances, or what events in this act have brought about this change? Has Miller accomplished it convincingly or do you think that he has manipulated characters and incidents unrealistically in order to produce a desired result?

Again, a few detailed explanations are needed:

The reading of fortunes *(Hathorne):* the foretelling of people's futures

Cain were an upright man *(Parris):* Cain was an honest man. In the Bible (Genesis 4) Cain the son of Adam, by killing his brother Abel, committed the first murder

Remember what the angel Raphael said *(Proctor):* the story of Tobias and the angel occurs in the Book of Tobit in the Apocrypha, a collection of works resembling the Bible but the authenticity of which is doubted

Clap me for contempt of a hearing *(Corey):* arrest me for refusing to obey a legal proceeding which does not have the full authority of a court

ipso facto (Danforth): (Latin) by that very fact itself; a legal phrase

A very augur bit will now be turned into your souls *(Danforth):* emphasising the rigour of his investigation, Danforth compares it to the sharp-pointed drill used to bore into wood or metal

There might also be a dragon with five legs in my house *(Proctor):* by choosing so obviously fictitious an example, Proctor mockingly belittles Parris's idea of probability. In an earlier version Proctor had said 'There might also be two golden candlesticks ...', but no doubt Miller changed this so as to emphasise that Proctor wishes only to ridicule Parris; the candlesticks reference would reopen his long-standing quarrel with Parris and would suggest that he loses no opportunity of pursuing this

Wastin' his time at the shovelboard *(Elizabeth):* shovelboard was a game played (probably for gambling) in taverns. It involved striking a disc with the hand so as to propel it across a marked board

They're gulling you *(Proctor):* They're making a fool of you by their deceit

Lucifer *(Danforth):* another name for the Devil

Act Four

Three months have passed and it is now autumn. In a cell in Salem jail Herrick, the marshal, rouses Sarah Good and Tituba from sleep. Sarah thinks he is the Devil but Tituba knows better. They tell him that they plan to fly with the Devil to the warmth of Barbados in the West Indies, away from the cold of Massachusetts. Herrick shares his alcohol with them to warm them, and Tituba mistakes a cow's lowing for the call of the Devil. He hurries them away to another cell as Danforth, Hathorne, and Cheever enter.

Danforth is annoyed that Hale, who has returned to Salem, is being allowed access to the prison, and Herrick, who has been drinking heavily, explains that Parris has authorised this. Reproving Herrick for his drunkenness, and complaining of the smell in the jail, Danforth sends Herrick to fetch Parris. To Hathorne's suggestion that Hale may have been preaching in Andover Danforth replies cryptically that nothing must be said about Andover. Danforth is puzzled at Parris's new friendship with Hale, and Hathorne attributes Parris's emotional behaviour to a disturbed mind. Cheever, however, suggests that, with so many men now imprisoned, many cows have broken loose and the disputes over the ownership of these beasts may have distressed the minister.

The Parris who now enters is a much less aggressive man than when we last saw him. He tells Danforth and Hathorne of the good work Hale is doing in urging Rebecca, Martha, and others to confess and save their lives. He seems to hint that, if Hale succeeds in this, Danforth should reprieve the women. Abigail and Mercy Lewis have fled from Salem three days earlier, taking with them all Parris's money, which they have stolen. Parris is upset at this but even more afraid that the Deputy Governor will be angry with him. Abigail, he fears, has escaped by ship on hearing the news from Andover, but Danforth assures him that all has been put right there. Parris knows that there has been a rebellion in Andover against the witchhunting activities of the court there and is afraid that the same will happen in Salem. The townspeople had accepted the hanging of a few good-for-nothings but, he argues, would be outraged if Rebecca were to be executed, especially if she behaved on the scaffold in her usual godly manner. Hathorne reminds him that Rebecca has been found guilty, but Parris recommends postponing the hangings. Danforth is opposed to this, but he seems to see the force of Parris's suggestion that, by waiting until Hale has secured a confession from one of them, they can convince the people that all the accused are equally guilty. Danforth offers to spend the night himself in trying to obtain a confession from whichever prisoner Parris thinks most likely to give way, but Parris is troubled at the small number of people present when he excommunicated Proctor and at the attempt that has been made on his own life. Clearly the townspeople are becoming increasingly critical of the authorities.

The Reverend Hale now arrives but when Danforth congratulates him he has to admit that none will confess. Hale wants Danforth to pardon them all, but Danforth refuses because others have already been executed for the same offence. Nor will he agree to any postponement, fearing that this would be interpreted as weakness on his part. He threatens to put down any attempt at rebellion by mass executions if necessary, rather than seek to avert rebellion by pardoning the seven already under sentence.

The only prisoner with whom Hale has not talked is Proctor, who is now kept in chains for having assaulted the marshal and who, beyond eating a little, shows no interest in life. He has not seen his pregnant wife for three months, and Danforth orders them both to be brought before him. Hale again suggests postponement which he thinks the people would attribute to mercy, not to weakness, but Danforth is adamant. This, warns Hale, may provoke rebellion when there is so much distress and disorder in Salem already. Asked whether he has preached in Andover, he replies that they do not need him there, implying that Andover has put an end to the witchhunting. Sourly he describes his own work at present as encouraging Christians to save their lives by falsely confessing to what they have not done. A strong sense of guilt has brought him near to breakdown, but he controls himself as Elizabeth enters.

Her child is not expected for another six months, she says, and Danforth assures her that they do not seek her life. He invites Hale to reason with her in the hope that she will confess, and Hale reminds her that her husband is to be hanged the next day. He would like to save Proctor, he says, though this involves advising Christians to tell lies. Hathorne and Danforth protest angrily at this insistence on the inno-cence of the condemned, but Hale is very worried at the harm his religion has caused in Salem. Better no religion at all, he tells Elizabeth, than a religion that leads only to bloodshed and death. He tries to persuade her to influence her husband so that Proctor may save his own life by a false confession, but Elizabeth quietly tells him how wrong that would be. Hale replies that she cannot be certain what God wants her to do, and Danforth plays on her emotions by suggesting that she is indifferent to her husband's fate. She agrees to talk to Proctor but gives no guarantee of what she will say.

Proctor is brought in, chained. Danforth urges him to save himself, Parris offers him drink, but Proctor is silent until they leave him alone with Elizabeth. He asks tenderly how she and the children are, he confirms her suspicion that he has been tortured, and tells her he is to die. In reply to a question from him, she says that, although many have 'confessed', Rebecca is steadfast in her refusal to do so and is quite reconciled to death.

Giles Corey, she tells him, is dead but not by hanging. Knowing that his sons could not inherit his property if he were condemned, he had refused to give any answer to the charge. When he was tortured in order to be forced to plead either guilty or not guilty, his only answer had been to tell his torturers to add more stones to the weight they were piling on him, and so they pressed him to death, but his sons inherited his farm.

Both Proctor and his wife pay tribute to Corey's courage, but Proctor then tells her that he thinks of making a 'confession'. Much as she wants him to live, she will not advise him what to do. He asks whether Martha Corey has confessed but is told she has not. He suggests that, as his moral failings are already publicly known, another lie to save himself can hardly damage his reputation any more, but Elizabeth reminds him that something has prevented his confessing up to this time. Attributing his silence hitherto only to spite, he asks her forgiveness for what he is about to do, but she expresses doubt as to whether he will forgive himself. She tells him that he is a good man and that her coldness was to blame for his unfaithfulness, but he will not hear of this. As she apologises again for the sense of her own unworthiness that made her inadequate as a wife to so good a husband, Hathorne enters to ask for his decision.

To Hathorne's amazement Proctor asks for his life. As Hathorne summons the others to witness this miracle, Proctor repeats that, unlike Rebecca, he is no saint and thus can afford to lie, but it is plain to us that he is not really convinced by his own arguments, and that Elizabeth cannot give her approval to what he is doing. The others return triumphantly, Danforth demanding that it be set down in writing for the public good. Answering his cross-examination, Proctor is curtly admitting having met the Devil when Rebecca Nurse, very weak, comes in. She hears his evidence with pained surprise and refuses Danforth's invitation to make a confession herself. When Proctor refuses to incriminate his friends by saying that he saw them in the Devil's company, Danforth becomes angry and tries to coerce him into naming others, but Proctor will not. Hale and Parris persuade Danforth to accept Proctor's statement as it stands and reluctantly Danforth asks Proctor to sign it. Equally reluctantly, Proctor signs, but immediately snatches the paper back.

If God and these witnesses have seen him sign it, he protests, that is enough without having it publicly displayed to the town. Conscious that he has, by his lie, betrayed his friends and his children, he will not allow Danforth to keep the document. Unable to understand his reasoning, Danforth demands an explanation. Proctor realises that he cannot persist with this dishonesty and tears up the paper. Aghast, Hale warns him that he will hang, but Proctor is quite prepared to accept this in his newfound awareness that he cannot gratify his enemies by betraying his own principles. Danforth orders the execution of both Proctor and Rebecca, who stoically attributes her weakness to not having breakfasted. Hale and Parris continue to plead with Elizabeth to prevent Proctor from condemning himself but she, knowing that his mind is made up to do what is right, steadfastly refuses to deny him his reputation by interfering, and the play ends with a drumroll heralding the execution as a new day breaks.

NOTES

The questions the reader should ask about this act are these: what purpose is served by the events preceding the first entry of Danforth? What changes have taken place in the main characters since Act Three, and what further changes take place during this act? At the end of Act Three it was obvious that Proctor was doomed: is this act, then, superfluous, or how does it complete our understanding of the events as a whole? How does Miller sustain our interest if, in fact, we expect things to end as they do? Is it true to say that the play ends on a note of unrelieved gloom?

It is a measure of the simple and direct eloquence of this final act that nothing in it calls for the kind of explanation or glossing needed by the earlier acts. .

Part 3

Commentary

Historical background

The fiction and the facts

Prefixed to *The Crucible* is a note by Miller beginning with the words 'This play is not history'. It does, however, deal with historical events and with characters who, even though Miller recommends us to regard them as his own inventions, had an historical existence. Its author went to considerable trouble to familiarise himself with the source material and to dramatise it as faithfully as he could. What, then, is the relationship between history and drama, fact and fiction? In the note Miller claims that 'the reader will discover here *the essential nature* of one of the strangest and most awful chapters in human history'. The words italicised are crucial: what would have been the difference if Miller had written 'the essential facts' or 'the whole truth'?

Had he done so, we would have been entitled—perhaps even obliged—to go back to his original sources, to compare them with the play, and to see whether he had taken liberties with the original, adding something that was not there, or omitting something that was. By promising us only 'the essential nature' of the episode he implies that he has not falsified or wilfully distorted the original but has focused only on the aspects of it that seem to him of perennial significance. The reader should ask himself whether the play raises issues that are at all applicable to his place and his time, and whether this helps to make more real or more credible to him the behaviour of the historical characters represented.

From the original records, from Marion Starkey's book referred to already, or from the more recent *Witchcraft at Salem* by Chadwick Hansen*, we can see how closely Miller has followed his sources. The original John Proctor seems to have been a rougher, less sensitive man than his counterpart in the play, and the other characters vary in small details from their originals, but the most significant change Miller makes is in respect of Abigail. Hansen refers to her as being only twelve years of age, whereas in *The Crucible* she is obviously several years

*Published by George Braziller, New York, 1969

older. As students of drama, not as historians, we need to ask why Miller made this change, and what dramatic purpose it serves. Before returning to this, however, we can usefully fill in more of the historical background.

Witchcraft in New England

A belief in witchcraft had been held for centuries throughout the world and was still current in Europe. Its existence in Massachusetts was encouraged by three factors to which Miller calls attention explicitly in the 'background essay' and implicitly in the play. The first white settlers had only arrived in New England in 1620 and Salem had been in existence for only forty years or so by 1692, so its inhabitants would naturally feel isolated, insecure, and vulnerable. The hostility of the native Indians intensified this: the Puritans were used to their attacks (Abigail refers to her parents having been killed before her eyes by Indians) and spoke of the woods as the Devil's territory (which is why Tituba and the girls had gone there). Indians for them were the Devil's agents. Moreover, having emigrated to America to escape persecution for their religious beliefs, the Puritans tended to expect persecution of one sort or another: indeed, they almost welcomed it as evidence that God was testing them and that by facing such adversity staunchly they were glorifying God and making their own community an outstanding example to others.

That community was of course a theocracy: that is to say, there was the closest possible identity between church and state in the government of the country. Thus if witchcraft threatened the religious order it automatically threatened the state at the same time. This explains the intensity of their reaction to any suspicion of witchcraft. When Parris claims that Proctor is challenging 'authority' there is no need to define whether it is religious or civil authority he is attacking for they are almost synonymous.

Hansen's researches convince him that witchcraft was not only believed in but was actually practised in Massachusetts.* He identifies three kinds of witchcraft: first, 'white magic' or the use of charms and spells to bring good luck to the user and to protect him from evil spirits; second, 'black magic' or the malicious use of charms and spells to harm others (for example, by sticking a pin into an image of another person in the belief that this will magically cause physical pain or death to that person, which is what Elizabeth is accused of in the play); third, the entering into a pact with the Devil, whereby the witch promises to

*Miller had made the same point in his *Collected Plays*, p.250

serve him in return for certain favours and magic powers. Hansen does not ask us to believe that any of these forms of witchcraft was actually capable of producing the desired effects, but he reminds us that people who believe in witchcraft can very easily persuade themselves of its effectiveness. Adolescents in particular may frighten themselves into believing that they have seen some supernatural phenomenon, or that symptoms of illness may indeed have been caused by an enemy. In extreme cases they may unintentionally induce such symptoms in themselves by a process that we would now call psychosomatic. The hysteria that such people manifest is, Hansen suggests, an identifiable clinical condition of ill-health and not merely the over-emotional state that we describe, in everyday usage, as hysteria.

Hansen, in short, challenges the modern rationalist interpretation of the events in Salem. Rationalists do not themselves believe in witchcraft, and so will not accept that intelligent people in 1692 should have believed in it either. From this point of view, of course, the behaviour of the girls who accused the 'witches' becomes malicious play-acting, the people who fear it are simple, superstitious, and credulous, and the authorities who bring people to trial and condemn them for witchcraft do so from a cynical desire to exploit the situation to their own advantage and to strengthen their control over the populace.

Which of these interpretations does *The Crucible* support? How firmly does it support either? How do they help our understanding of the theme of the play? To these and other questions the reader should form his own answer and then test it against the discussion of them that occurs later.

From all sources it is quite clear that, as in the play, it was Judge Hathorne who was particularly vigorous in prosecuting the suspected witches, and particularly severe in his interrogation of them; some of that interrogation occurs in the play in almost the same words as in the original. A nineteenth-century descendant of the judge was the American novelist Nathaniel Hawthorne; in the introduction to his best-known novel, *The Scarlet Letter* (1850), he talks, with strong feelings of guilt, about his ancestor's harshness and cruelty. The Reverend Hale figures less prominently in Hansen's account than in Miller's, but in fact he wrote a book entitled *A Modest Inquiry into the Nature of Witchcraft* (1702). Although he admits that he and his colleagues may have been over-zealous, he states, quite unambiguously, 'I observed in the prosecution of these affairs, that there was in the Justices, Judges and others concerned, a conscientious endeavour to do the thing that was right'. Would we say the same of their counterparts in *The Crucible*?

The themes of the play

Good and evil

In the Introduction Miller looks back at criticisms made of the play on its first appearance four years earlier. Some critics had complained that he had over-emphasised the malice and cruelty of the prosecutors, thus giving the impression that they were totally evil, monsters rather than human beings. Miller's reply is that the original records show them in exactly that light, that his presentation of Danforth, for example, makes him more human than the sources do, and that if he were to re-write *The Crucible* he would intensify, rather than reduce, the evil nature of these men.

This raises fundamental questions, our individual answers to which will condition our understanding and our interpretation of the play. First, are we sufficiently convinced that the behaviour of the prosecutors in the play is credible? Obviously, if we think that human beings could never behave like that, the play will not affect us as deeply as it would if we find their behaviour recognisably true to life. Second, what does the play in its existing form suggest to us about the nature and effect of evil in the sequence of events that it depicts? There is no doubt that Danforth, Parris, Hathorne, and to some extent Hale, are responsible, by the severity of their attempts to stamp out witchcraft, for many deaths and much misery. Even if we believe them to be misguided and over-zealous rather than deliberately wicked, most of the evil arises from their actions. They oversimplify the issues into black and white (as in Danforth's belief that people who are not supporting him are therefore totally opposed to him).

However black Miller makes Danforth and his colleagues seem, though, he is careful not to make the other characters (except perhaps Rebecca Nurse) wholly white and blameless. Proctor and Corey, by their hot-tempered impulsiveness, put their wives and eventually themselves in danger; Proctor is, of course, an adulterer; Elizabeth may have been less affectionate as a wife than she might have been; the antagonisms between the characters that existed even before the witchcraft panic are based on petty jealousies and often on quite trivial things (Proctor's hostility to Parris and his dislike of Putnam, Corey's readiness to take his neighbours to law on the slightest excuse), but they have helped to create an atmosphere of enmity and mistrust in which the accusations of witchcraft can do the maximum harm. Miller complains, in his discussion of this play, of the twentieth-century unwillingness to believe that people can be consciously dedicated to evil: it may be said that, by so deliberately demonstrating that nobody is completely good, he makes it harder for us to accept that anybody can be completely bad.

It is perhaps surprising that when Miller is discussing the forces of evil in this play he concentrates on the judges and almost entirely ignores Abigail. This may well be because, as the 'background essay' shows, he is so predominantly concerned with the social and political aspects of his theme. In the Introduction he expresses his horror at 'the notion that conscience was no longer a private matter but one of state administration'. To that extent he may be accused of simplifying the issues involved into a conflict between a would-be totalitarian state and an independently-minded people. The postscript to the play ascribes to these events the destruction of the power of theocracy in Massachusetts. Historically the whole issue was much more complex than that, but more significant for our purposes is the demonstrable difference between what Miller says in his comments on the play and what the play says in itself.

The treatment of the suspects, in historical fact and in the play, was undeniably cruel, but that cruelty only came into being because witchcraft was suspected and a kind of mass hysteria ensued. Now in the play all this is attributable to the deliberate actions of Abigail, aided by her friends. Had she at any point said in public what she says to Proctor in Act One in private, there could be no excuse for the persecution at all. That she does not do this is explained by Miller as primarily due to her malicious desire for vengeance on Elizabeth and for marriage to Proctor. Admittedly the situation quickly gets too much out of control for her to be able to retract, but hers is the chief responsibility for starting and for intensifying the panic. She is thus the most positively evil character in the play, yet not only does Miller ignore her in discussing the play's moral implications but he also prompts us to see Proctor's adultery with this young and emotional girl as some excuse for her subsequent behaviour. In the Introduction he admits that it was Abigail's role in the story that first awakened his interest and says that his 'central impulse for writing at all was not the social but the interior psychological question'. The apparent inconsistencies in his accounts of his own motivation can best be explained by returning to two questions raised earlier.

First, by deliberately making Abigail an adolescent rather than the twelve-year-old that she is in the sources, he introduces into the story a sexual element that some critics see as intended to give only a spurious kind of excitement that will engage the audience's attention. Her infatuation with Proctor, however, is a crucial strand in the play, but her psychology is less central to it than Miller implies. Later, in a fuller discussion of her character, it will be suggested that the scene in the wood with Proctor, added and then removed, has the effect of making her psychologically more complex and in some ways a more sympathetic character: its removal makes her role more evil and re-focuses our attention on the public rather than the personal dimension of the story. Her relations with Proctor, though, do give her a very plausible motive for exploiting the situation that arises from the girls' nocturnal pranks in the woods, and at this point we must reconsider the way in which the play encourages us to view witchcraft.

Witchcraft in *The Crucible*

Miller would seem to disagree with Hansen's view somewhat and to take a more rationalistic attitude, but we need to look carefully at the way in which the play determines our thinking on this question. At the very beginning Parris is convinced that his daughter's illness is due to witchcraft. Some critics, in the light of what happens later, take it for granted that Betty is only feigning illness, but there doesn't seem to be anything in the text to support this. Indeed, if she were, is Abigail likely to talk so intimately to Proctor in Betty's presence? Certainly if it was obvious to the audience that Betty is only pretending, the opening act, and indeed the play as a whole, would lose much of its impact in the theatre. There are two reasons why we should be kept in doubt on this question. If we regard the people of Salem as foolish, superstitious rustics incapable of seeing through the deceptions practised on them, we cannot respect as we should their obvious terror at the events that overtake them or the courage with which they confront them. If, rationalists that we probably are, we can be induced to suspend for as long as possible our total disbelief in witchcraft and to entertain the possibility that something very strange is at work in Salem, we can enter better into the spirit of the play.

If we accept that Betty really is ill, the first Act gains in theatrical tension and also establishes something not far removed from Hansen's theory. Her illness is not caused directly by witchcraft but may well be a ten-year-old's over-excited response to the events in the wood and a neurotic guilt at having participated in what she believes to be forbidden and occult rites; in other words, it is a psychosomatically-induced illness caused not by witchcraft but by a belief in witchcraft. If the conduct of the girls is merely calculated play-acting, the response of the adults to it becomes almost contemptible; similarly, Mary Warren's inability to pretend to faint when so much depends on her doing so becomes incomprehensible unless her earlier faintings are also seen as psycho-somatic. In short, the play does not require us to believe in witchcraft but, like Hansen's argument, to accept the fact that, in circumstances other than our own, people who are by no means stupid, unintelligent, or godless, might very well believe in it.

If we accept that, the play can become more, rather than less, disturbing. Abigail's anger at Betty in Act One is merely spiteful if she knows her to be feigning: the stage directions, when Betty briefly recovers consciousness, however, make it clear that the girls are gen-uinely frightened by the turn events have taken and fearful that their games have somehow really released a force outside their control. This interpretation of the play suggests that a force of evil was generated in Salem by a combination of circumstances for which no one person was wholly responsible but for which none was wholly guiltless either; and that those circumstances were then deliberately exploited by some people more unscrupulous than others. Evil flourished for a time because many well-intentioned people could not see how to stop it, and, indeed, without wishing to, often made the situation worse.

Moreover, this happened in the seventeenth-century New England theocracy. If such harm could come to people who had tried to form themselves into 'a community of saints' (to use a phrase of the period), it is an alarming indication of human vulnerability to evil. It suggests, too, that religion is not necessarily able successfully to withstand evil, and that evil may actually be done by people who believe themselves to be acting in accordance with their religious beliefs. This is why Hale is so necessary in this play. Even if we wish to see Danforth and Hathorne as consciously wicked, Miller is very careful to make Hale a likeable, conscientious, but fundamentally misguided man who comes to realise that faith itself can, in an excess of zeal, create results that are indisputably evil.

Evil and tragedy

Miller's comments on how he might rewrite the play prompt one last question: what would be the difference between the play as we have it and the play as Miller suggests it might be? Miller argues that modern drama is weakened by what he calls our inability to conceive of Iago. He is referring to Shakespeare's *Othello*, where the villainous Iago, jealous of the noble and heroic Othello, wickedly and successfully schemes to destroy him by deliberately playing on the one weakness in Othello's character, his assumption that everyone else is as honest as he is himself. There is no doubt that Shakespearean tragedy affects us in a way that much modern drama does not. The ancient Greek philosopher Aristotle (384–322 BC) taught that tragedy performed the useful function of purging the audience's emotions of pity and fear. *Othello* certainly arouses pity for the hero and his wife, and fear of the evil that Iago represents, but by the end of the play Iago is killed in punishment and our admiration for Othello's greatness counteracts our pity, so that tragedy has the paradoxical effect of restoring and perhaps strengthening our faith in man.

Now even if Miller were to rewrite *The Crucible* he could hardly achieve this kind of effect, however wicked he made the prosecutors, because the historical facts of the story do not allow the prosecutors to be punished with the poetic justice that enables Shakespeare to kill Iago, and, admirable as John Proctor is in many respects, he cannot, as a simple Massachusetts farmer, be given the heroic stature of a great leader and public figure like Othello. All this is relevant to *The Crucible* only because it shows us, by contrast, an essential aspect of the play that may indeed be one of its virtues. *The Crucible* does not end with the clearcut finality of *Othello* or the unmistakeable restoration of order. The final stage directions have Elizabeth near collapse and Hale weeping openly; Danforth and Hathorne have not been defeated, although Proctor's courage is an important challenge to them; and the only ray of hope for the future is symbolised by the shaft of dawn sunlight that falls on Elizabeth. The effect of this ending is not uplifting in the way that tragedy is, but neither is it totally depressing, and in one sense it may be more realistic. By not embodying evil in one Iago-like figure and suggesting its elimination by his death, *The Crucible* is a reminder of more insidious forms of evil that can be brought about by ordinary men. Such forms of evil are perhaps more obviously discernible in the modern world than is Iago's, and in that sense more frightening. What, then, the play forces us to ask, can we hope to bring against such evil?

Personal integrity

Proctor's most important decision is taken when he tears up his 'confession' at the end with the words 'How may I live without my name? I have given you my soul: leave me my name!'. Because the confession is a lie he believes himself damned even if only Danforth knows what he has done, but, if the confession is published, then his reputation is destroyed among people who had respected him and—what matters more to Proctor—he knows that he can no longer respect himself. It is because Elizabeth knows what this means to him that she will not presume to advise or criticise him. He must make his own moral decisions independently, and when, in the closing minutes of the play, Hale again urges her to plead with her husband, she still refuses. The struggle nearly breaks her, but her husband's honour is more important to her than his life, as it is to him. 'He have his goodness now', she says at the end, 'God forbid I take it from him!'

Proctor's 'name' is more than merely his reputation: it is his honour, his loyalty to himself, his personal integrity. Similarly, it is Elizabeth's sense of her own integrity that gives her the courage to do what she knows to be right. At the beginning of the play, when Parris is uncertain whether he can really trust Abigail, the question that he asks her is 'Your name in the town—it is entirely white, is it not?'. Revising the scene, Miller significantly allowed Abigail to make even more use of this particular form of words to protest her innocence. Puritans were always expected to lead lives that could be seen by others to be blameless, so this anxiety to keep one's name beyond reproach is historically appropriate. Yet, beset by the evil that develops all round them, these Puritans derive from their religion less moral support than might be expected.

This is partly because, again with historical accuracy, Miller represents the community of 1692 as less idealistic than the original settlers, more disposed to quarrelling among themselves. The fact that the trouble broke out in the house of a minister, and the attitude of the authorities to the outbreak, must have caused some loss of confidence in the clergy; some weakening of religious faith must be expected also when ordinary people are confronted by events so inexplicable and so terrifying.

Moral uncertainty

The real John Hale spoke of 'a conscientious endeavour to do the thing that was right'. This sums up very well the conduct of the Coreys, the Nurses, and especially the Proctors in this play; it may even apply to Danforth, Hale, Hathorne, Parris, and even Putnam, if we take a charitable view. The only person to whom it cannot apply is Abigail. Yet even the 'good' characters have real difficulty in being certain of exactly what *is* right.

The language of the play gives a clear clue to their attitude. The repetition of the phrase 'I think' in their speeches is indicative of this. For example, in Act Two, Elizabeth says in successive speeches, 'The town's gone wild, I think', 'I think you must go to Salem, John. I think so', and, speaking of the court, 'I think they must be told'. To this

Proctor replies 'I'll think on it', and 'I think it is not easy to prove she's fraud'. All this suggests, not a limited vocabulary on the part of characters or author, but the uncertainty they feel as to exactly what their duty is. If they were more sure, the conflict within themselves would be less dramatic, the play would be less effective, and the audience would feel less involved in the dilemma. These are ordinary people who wish to obey their consciences but are not sure what conscience requires of them. Conscientiously, they are trying to do, not what they *feel* to be right, but what they *think* to be right, and that is more difficult to determine.

After his 'confession' Proctor is asked to name others whom he has seen in the Devil's company. In slightly different words this was regularly asked of people in the 1950s by Congressional investigators, but Proctor's instant and complete refusal is more than a lesson for the times: it is quite consistent with his own character and his moral code. He knows that he must not betray others, and, when circumstances force him to face that, he moves quickly and quite consciously to the realisation that he must not betray himself either. Thinking has at last resulted in knowing, and protecting his name and his integrity is all that matters now.

The title of the play

A crucible is a pot in which metals are melted down, usually in order to purify them by separating out baser elements that have become mixed with them. Using this as the title of his play, Miller implies a concern with a process of purging by fire. This is a familiar metaphor for man's spiritual improvement as a result of exposure to a period of great strain and temptation. Thus it identifies the spiritual development of John Proctor as the play's central theme.

An alternative explanation might be that Salem in 1692 was the crucible from which there emerged a purified American democracy. Given Miller's interest in the historical and political aspects of the story, and his use of such phrases as 'the power of theocracy in Massachusetts was broken', this is by no means implausible, but the structure of the play would suggest that this association is only secondary.

There may, incidentally, be a slightly grim irony in this title. In popular belief, a normal piece of a witch's equipment was a cauldron in which all kinds of unpleasant ingredients were brewed together for purposes of black magic. Shakespeare's witches in *Macbeth* use a cauldron, and in Act One of *The Crucible* it is established that the girls had a kettle with them in the woods for a similar purpose. Miller's title may thus imply that a cauldron may become a crucible, that out of attempted evil good may come: this would be quite consistent with the themes of the play.

The structure of the play

There are two ways in which a play or a novel is seen to have a unity and a completeness. One is plot: the events of the story should be so presented as to have a perceptible beginning, a logical development, and a convincing end. Part 2 should have established *The Crucible's* unity of plot. There should also be a structural unity, by which is meant the way in which the narrative is constructed, the relationship and balance between the acts, as well as between the elements within them, and the pattern that the whole play makes. The summaries, and the questions following them, give some sense of this, but the overall structure will now be discussed and related to the themes.

The play begins vigorously, the action being set in motion even before the exposition. No time is wasted in the old convention of having two characters hold a conversation that is intended only to convey information to a passive, listening audience. Parris's anxiety over Betty and his cross-examining of Abigail ensure that the action is under way from the moment the curtain rises, while at the same time our attention is directed to the unexplained events of the previous evening. The background of quarrels among the townspeople is gradually revealed in the dialogue between Proctor and Parris and in that between Corey and Putnam. Proctor's earlier relationship with Abigail emerges equally naturally in their conversation with each other.

However, drama often depends for its effectiveness more on the withholding of information than on the imparting of it, and our curiosity as to the events of the previous night is stimulated by being kept unsatisfied. Miller's first version of the play had begun with a scene in the woods which was dropped in production because it added to the cost but was not essential to the action. Indeed, if it removed at the outset the ambiguity surrounding this incident it would weaken the first act by destroying its suspense. This Miller builds up by allowing the characters to make conflicting statements about what took place, and by not indicating which account we ought to believe. It is also a useful way of reminding us that it was only on this flimsy, unreliable, and very questionable evidence that the whole witch-hunt was based.

Act One establishes an atmosphere of tension, a mood of uncertainty, and an impression of a very disturbed township. As many as thirteen characters are introduced, and their comings and goings create a sense of excited activity. Their anxiety over the strange happenings, their superstitious credulity, and their suspicions of each other prepare us for the events that are to follow; Betty's irrational behaviour and Tituba's breakdown under questioning create a dramatic tension that culminates vividly in the final hysterical chanting. The abruptness of this ending, very effective in the theatre, serves another purpose too. Everything happens too quickly for us to be quite clear why Abigail has joined in the denunciations, and the stage directions deliberately offer no comment beyond suggesting, by the use of words like 'inspired' and 'enraptured', that she may have genuinely experienced a religious conversion. We are, in short, hardly more certain than the characters themselves whether the girls are deceiving us or whether some supernatural force really is at work, and the unexpectedness of the outburst intensifies this. The only moment of quiet in the whole act comes with the entrance of Hale, yet we are not entirely assured that he is as stable and as sound a personality as he seems. Our interest, in short, is sustained by uncertainty and by the desire for some resolution of our doubts in the ensuing acts.

After the bustle and excitement of Act One, the second act opens on a very quiet note but we are quickly made aware of the strained relations between Proctor and his wife. Whenever it appears about to be eased, something accidentally happens to increase it. In the same way, later in the act, we realise the danger Elizabeth is in, and every time there seems some hope of averting it something happens that makes the danger worse. Suspense is achieved in this act by alternately raising our hopes and disappointing them. The dramatic tension mounts, the intensity of the quarrels between the characters growing steadily until this act also ends on a note of hysteria.

For almost half of Act Two the Proctors and Mary are the only characters on stage. They are then joined by Hale, but Mary leaves, so there are still only three. In Act One more characters were involved and the quickly changing combinations in which they appeared on stage contributed to the sense of bustle. There is a comparable episode here (between Cheever's entrance and the arrest of Elizabeth), but it is much shorter and the act ends with Proctor and Mary alone, whereas Act One had built up to a final scene with eight people. Proctor is on stage for the whole of Act Two, Elizabeth for the greater part of it. It is on this pair, then, that our attention is by now firmly focused, though the conversations, and particularly the references to Rebecca, keep us aware of a world outside and its escalating panic which eventually breaks into the relative calm of the Proctor household.

Although Abigail does not appear in this act, the frequent allusions to her guarantee her a metaphorical and distinctly ominous presence throughout. It was after this act that Miller in revising the play introduced the subsequently abandoned scene between Abigail and Proctor. Its contribution to the characterisation of Abigail has been mentioned, but as a reminder of her existence it is superfluous, it adds nothing to the action, and structurally it is a distraction. Not only is it implausible (Proctor would not have sought such an interview after Elizabeth's arrest), but in a play composed of four acts of roughly equal length the interpolation of this brief dialogue disturbs the rhythm and the balance. Proctor's confrontation must now be publicly with the town, not in private with Abigail, for he has finished with her: better, therefore, to move direct from the end of Act Two to the public scene of the court.

The keynote of Act Three is confusion. It opens noisily with the ejection of Corey from the courtroom, it ends like its predecessors on a tempestuous climax of hysteria. The quarrelling and argument that separate these two events are more continuous than in the other acts, no less bitter, but in some respects more rational, less emotional but theatrically very compelling. If the audience was ever in any doubt, they now realise that the outcome of this play must be tragic. The hope-and-disappointment pattern of the previous act is repeated but with more far-reaching implications: opportunities constantly arise for the whole problem to be cleared up satisfactorily, but these are always frustrated, and frustrated with ever more serious consequences. Yet the opportunities are lost, not by deliberate wickedness, but by accident. It is an act of interruptions, of explanations tragically delayed.

Danforth is trying to conduct an enquiry, but he is constantly distracted from one problem to another by chance. Martha's trial is interrupted by Corey's well-meant intervention which Danforth tries to investigate: Nurse's attempt to show him the truth is prevented by the arrival of Proctor and Mary, but their evidence is sidetracked, first by Parris, then by the disclosure of Elizabeth's pregnancy, then by the decision to arrest the ninety-one witnesses, and finally by Corey's quarrel with Putnam. Throughout all this, Mary, waiting to give evidence, becomes more and more upset, so that, at last asked to speak, she loses confidence. Abigail's attempt to exploit this exasperates Proctor who loses his temper and attacks Abigail in a moment of sudden physical action.

This is the turning-point of the play, because after this he must disclose his own guilt and whatever he then does is bound to be turned to his disadvantage. The skill with which Miller manoeuvres him into this position deserves credit for its unobtrusiveness: everything happens naturally, one thing leads to another, the characters all inadvertently contribute to their own downfall. Abigail's schemes need never have succeeded if enough of the other characters had kept their heads, but they have muddled themselves towards a point of no return without any wish to do so, and now nothing short of a miracle can retrieve the situation.

As human beings we may wish such a miracle were possible; as playgoers we know by the end of Act Three, from the structure and the tone of the play, how inconceivable it would be. Two criticisms are sometimes made of *The Crucible*: first, that the action is really complete by the end of Act Three and the final act serves only to prolong the agony unnecessarily; second, that Miller seems undecided as to whether he is concentrating on the tragedy of Salem or the tragedy of John Proctor. The second of these arguments is better answered first.

Once the first act has established the witch-hunting atmosphere, the next two acts focus increasingly on the Proctors, subordinating to them the stories of the Nurses and the Coreys. The opening scene of Act Four, however, confuses this temporarily. There is no valid reason for bringing back Tituba, and even less for introducing Sarah Good for the first time in person. The effect of this scene is uncertain; it is an unnecessary distraction, especially at this point, from the main movement of the play. Indeed, it is by no means clear whether it is designed to be grimly comic with its anti-climactic references to the arrival of the Devil, or whether it is pathetic in its revelation of the crazed, deluded state to which imprisonment has reduced the two women. It could be played in either way, but it is in any case too brief to make any real impact. If it is intended to re-widen the play's scope of reference, then it ought to lead to some resolution of their stories. Our expectation of this is raised, only to be disappointed. Miller is wiser in his rounding-off of the story of the Coreys by having it reported briefly (though with feeling) rather than staged. The fourth act would gain in simple directness and starkness of effect without this opening. If, however, Miller were trying to dramatise the whole Salem story (rather than to convey its 'essential nature' by focusing on the Proctors) the play would probably have had to contain many more such episodic scenes and to have become what is sometimes called a chronicle play. Its more concentrated four-act structure, with our attention increasingly brought to bear on the Proctors, brings it closer to tragedy, and this suggests one reason why the fourth act is essential.

In Act Three circumstances combine to doom Proctor: too quick an ending would have left us merely feeling sorry for him and for the way things have turned out. Act Four protracts the action only to heighten the tragedy by allowing Proctor to consent to his own death when he deliberately chooses adherence to moral principle rather than expediency. Thus Act Four earns for him from the audience the kind of respect that tragedy requires for its hero.

After the noise and anger of the preceding acts, Act Four is subdued in tone and essentially sober in its movement towards its inevitable end. The fanatical zeal of the persecutors has been broken by events, though they are not defeated. The changes in Parris and Hale since we last saw them give a new impetus to the action, while other elements in the plot (the Coreys' fate and Abigail's, for example) are quietly and briefly rounded off. The relationship between Proctor and his wife needs to be resolved after their last meeting in Act Three. Elizabeth's unfailing loyalty to and confidence in her husband are not unexpected, but it is dramatically right to represent them on stage and to demonstrate that they are not misplaced. The more intense clashes of the earlier acts give way to the debate between Danforth and Proctor about the latter's 'confession', but this, like the rest of the act, is relatively muted.

This debate represents, however, an effective piece of stagecraft to prevent the last act from dully moving along expected and predetermined lines. That Proctor should contemplate saving his life by this means takes the audience by surprise. The introduction of an unexpected turn of events at this point in a play is a device as old as Greek tragedy, as is also the reversal of it that follows almost immediately. George Bernard Shaw had used exactly the same device of the unexpected confession immediately recanted at exactly the same point in the action of his *Saint Joan* (1924), but this does not detract from its impact in *The Crucible*. It is entirely consistent with Proctor's character, which is often impulsive, and without this last-minute complication his acceptance of death would have seemed either too heroic or too passive. Thus the play is strengthened both as drama and as moral statement by this incident.

After all its frenzied conflict and debate, the play ends on a quiet note that must disappoint those who would have liked to see the persecutors punished with neat poetic justice, but it is the more convincing because it avoids that. It is a victory for the human spirit the more valuable for being so realistically limited a victory, and the stoic determination of both the Proctors relieves its gloom as positively as does the shaft of sunlight that coincides with Proctor's execution. This is no mere theatrical cliché. Proctor had condemned himself in Act Three when he admitted to adultery with Abigail but this had been done in an angry outburst and compounded by Elizabeth's well-meant lie on his behalf. Act Four establishes that three months in solitary confinement awaiting execution have strengthened his resolve more even than he himself realises, so that his final assertion of his own integrity is an even more impressive tribute to the indomitableness of the human will when challenged and tested over a significant period of time.

Is *The Crucible* a morality play?

Because of its concentration on moral issues and on the conflict between good and evil in the context of a Christian society, *The Crucible* is sometimes likened, by unsympathetic critics, to the 'morality plays' popular in medieval England. In the most famous of these, *Everyman*, the central character's name shows what he symbolises, and the other characters are similarly named after the abstract qualities that they personify. The story is plainly allegorical. Everyman is visited by Death who tells him to prepare for a journey, and he asks Fellowship, Kinsmen, and Goods to accompany him, only to find that Good-deeds alone can go with him. John Bunyan's *Pilgrim's Progress* (1678) might be described as a Puritan morality play in narrative form.

It could be said that, in *The Crucible*, Abigail represents Lust, Putnam is Greed, Parris is Credulity, Hale is Good Intentions, Elizabeth is Loyalty, and so on. This argument denigrates the play by implying that its characters, like those in the moralities, are symbols rather than people, that Miller's interest in them extends only to what he can make them represent, and that the play is more of a parable than a drama. What has already been said about the characters should challenge this as an over-simplification, and so should the following summaries of the main figures. Here they must be considered strictly as the fictitious creations of a dramatist and quite independent of their historical counterparts.

The characters

John Proctor

Although the central figure, Proctor is not idealised as a hero. He is a blunt, stubborn countryman, given to speaking his mind, rough and not excessively sensitive, yet capable of tenderness, especially towards women. In revising Act Two Miller added to Proctor's part the lines 'Lilacs have a purple smell. Lilac is the smell of nightfall, I think', as though to emphasise this. Proctor has been unfaithful to his wife, and Miller does not exonerate him; nevertheless, Proctor has tried to put an end to this before the action of the play begins, and his behaviour towards Elizabeth in Act Two shows remorse, as does his blustering self-defence in that act. Even in the additional scene with Abigail Miller allowed him no trace of affection for the girl, and he added to his part in Act One the specific statement, 'Abby, I never give [= gave] you hope to wait for me'. Proctor's adultery was probably no more than a moment of passion prompted by the impetuosity that characterises many of his other actions and speeches.

Yet he is undeniably a man of principle. His antagonism to Parris is consistent, if a little excessive, and he is clearly respected by his fellows. Slow in Act Two to agree to denounce Abigail, he never wavers once Elizabeth is arrested (another reason why the added scene with Abigail was better removed); a less heated and emotional attack on Abigail, however, might have been more efficacious but would have been less in character. His greatest moment comes in Act Four when he suddenly realises the importance of his own principles and his own integrity. His final speech to his wife had originally consisted only of the words 'Give them no tear! Show a stony heart and sink them with it!': the expanded version of that speech in the definitive text leaves us in no doubt as to how we are to think of him, as well as heightening the play's rhetoric at its climax. For the most part his language is simple, direct, colloquial, its bluffness occasionally enlivened by a hint of humour (as in his comments to Mary), but capable of effective and courageous use against his oppressors.

Elizabeth

Less complex than her husband, Elizabeth is still more than a mere embodiment of goodness. Both Abigail and Proctor speak of her coldness, and perhaps Miller ought to have done more in his presentation of her to belie this. She is gentle, devoted to her husband and her family: though her sons do not need to be brought into the action of the play, references to them indicate her maternal qualities, and the basic stability of the Proctors' marriage. The dignity and quiet wisdom with which she refutes Hale and Danforth, her social superiors, and the quality of the advice she gives her husband, indicate a seriousness of temperament as well as strength of mind. There is an occasional flash of anger, usually when Abigail's name is mentioned, as when she bids Hale question Abigail, not herself, about the Gospel. By no means indifferent to Proctor's adultery, she is more hurt by it than angered, and to others this can look like coldness. A comparison with Rebecca, however, will bring out the human side of Elizabeth, for Rebecca's role, necessarily a smaller one, is not developed much beyond an exemplary long-suffering goodness and patience.

Abigail

Miller has said that it was Abigail's role in the events that awakened his interest in the whole story, but his treatment of her is controlled though by no means dispassionate. A sensual adolescent, she has been flattered by Proctor's attentions and offended by their cessation. Her hostility to Elizabeth is a strong motive for the trouble she causes, but by no means the only one: a high-spirited sense of mischief and an enjoyment of the power she finds she can wield over her friends and others are also influential, and, although the point is not stressed, the brutal and violent death of her parents may have unsettled her.

The cancelled scene with Proctor in the woods, however, made her a more complex character by showing in her a streak of religiosity and a genuine belief in witchcraft that lead her to the conviction that she is being persecuted for being an agent of God. Proctor's attitude to her here makes it clear that we are to see her as deluded; he is moved to pity at her confusion, but is still determined to expose her. She, however, is pathetically sure that she can save him. It is an effective scene, but it belongs to a different play. To have retained it here would have required a complete alteration in the theme, for the complexity of this Abigail would have necessitated a much fuller development of her role in the play. Whether Miller sacrificed this scene in order to intensify the evil in the play or to emphasise its socio-political aspects is arguable. The Abigail who remains is a convincingly human and yet a frightening character, but her disappearance from the play after Act Three is a further indication of Miller's unwillingness to make her as crucial a character as he seems to have intended at first.

Danforth, Hathorne, and Parris

These three are best considered together, for they exemplify different kinds of authority. Hathorne is the simplest of them: an uncompromising but by no means unbelievable bigot, whose dedication to principle has destroyed his humanity and his imagination. Parris is at the other extreme: essentially a weak man, he mistakes for principle what is really self-protection against those whom he suspects quite rightly of despising him. For him authority is a defensive self-importance. There is a grotesqueness in his attempts to assert himself, his lack of perspective, and even his final change of heart which is occasioned more by fear than by enlightenment.

Between them comes Danforth: more intelligent than Parris, more imaginative than Hathorne and determined to do what he believes to be his duty. There are hints, however, that his firmness proceeds less from principle than from bewilderment. He does not understand what is happening, and, being something of a bully, relies on vigour of action to stop it. In Act Three particularly he could be convincingly played as a man less in command of the situation than he pretends to be and flustered by the speed of developments, yet not totally devoid of decent feeling. His willingness in Act Four, for example, to try to obtain a confession from one of the accused is not wholly attributable to self-interest.

Hale

Of all the characters it is Hale who seems to change the most, yet perhaps, like the others, he changes only in that the crisis strengthens his main characteristics. Hale's sincerity and his sense of public service remain constant: what changes is the end towards which they are directed. Initially convinced of the reality of witchcraft, he works assiduously to combat it by the only means he knows. Convinced of his error (and he is the only one of the prosecutors who is genuinely persuaded of the innocence of the accused), he still sees his first duty as the helping of others, but he sacrifices his principles in the process. It is not an easy role to portray, for he must not gain too much of our sympathy. Humane, intelligent, more open-minded than the others, he commands our respect, yet the logic of the play requires us to reject the position to which he finally comes. Seeing the harm that religious fanaticism can cause, he rejects not merely fanaticism but religion itself. His speech to Elizabeth in Act Four ('Let you not mistake your duty as I mistook my own . . .') is moving in its eloquence but is based on false premises, as Elizabeth reminds him in one very telling but quietly simple line: 'I think that be the Devil's argument'. This memorable exchange shows that Hale is making Proctor's mistake of preferring life to personal integrity, but where the simple farmer sees the moral error in that, the learned divine does not.

Minor characters

The other characters can be summed up more quickly. Their roles are simpler, their outlook less sophisticated, yet there are enough vivid and human touches in their behaviour and their lines for the actors to be able to make each of them lifelike and distinct from the others. Collectively they cover a representative spectrum of human strength and weakness; they suggest a credible community; and even they are less two-dimensional than the figures of the old morality plays.

Part 4

Hints for study

Visualising the play

Ideally the study of a play should begin by seeing it performed in the theatre and reading the text only after that. This will not often be possible, and it may in any case have its disadvantages. A strong production, whether good or bad, may impose, especially on an impressionable spectator, one interpretation of the play too authoritatively, making it more difficult for him to envisage alternative ways of presenting it. To make your first acquaintance with a play on the printed page, therefore, is not necessarily undesirable, but the text should be read always with performance in mind. Try to visualise it as clearly as possible, so that not only the scene but also the movements of the characters, and even their gestures and facial expressions, can be seen in the theatre of your mind.

In the case of *The Crucible* some preliminary familiarity with the domestic architecture, the costumes, and the general appearance of seventeenth-century New England would be an advantage, and could readily be acquired from the pages of an illustrated history of America (one such book is listed in Part 5). All the action of the play takes place indoors: a realistic setting, with the darkness of the low-beamed interiors, the unpretentious, sparse, and unornamented furniture, and the sombre simplicity of the clothing of the period, could contribute vividly to the oppressively enclosed, almost claustrophobic, atmosphere of the play. At the same time, the play's impact does not depend exclusively on a realistic, representational set; it has been presented to powerful effect on a completely bare stage.

In the theatre the sound of the play matters; it too needs to be experienced by the reader, preferably by reading it aloud. If this can be done by a group, each taking different parts, so much the better, but one person alone can still learn much about the play by practising the delivery of some of the key speeches aloud and considering how their maximum effect can be achieved.

Approaching the play through the characters

As in any other form of literary study, there is no substitute for a close and thorough knowledge of the text. These notes should help you towards that, but never use them instead of the text, only in conjunction with it; never treat them as exhaustive or definitive, but only as a stimulus to you in the forming of your own views on the play and its problems.

For example, you will quite probably wish to organise your own ideas about each of the characters: this is a natural step towards an understanding of the play, but it is not an end in itself. You will need to look at what the character does in the play, what that tells you about him, and what effect it has on the play's development. To take as an example some aspects of John Proctor: his adultery with Abigail puts a strain on his relationship with his wife (thus it affects another character), and it inhibits him from a prompt full denunciation of the girls as frauds (thereby affecting the plot). His known hostility to Parris makes the authorities uncertain of his motives (again this affects the plot) but shows him to be frank, open, and independent-minded (a deduction, from his conduct, about his personality). His change of heart at the end adds to the play's excitement (a link between character and structure) and also points the play's moral of the need for personal integrity (character contributing to theme).

Look also at what he says, first for the information it gives us (his criticism of Mary in Act Two focuses our attention on the peculiar way in which the court conducts its business); then for its indications of his personality (the unflinching courage of his exchanges with Danforth); and also for its style (the touches of humour that temper the anger of his reproofs of Mary). Style involves also the consideration of his more unusual, and particularly striking, turns of expression. In Act One he is good-humoured, blunt, but fundamentally serious ('I mean it solemnly, Rebecca: I like not the smell of this "authority"'). In Act Two the lyricism of his references to nature and lilacs gives way to coarse anger ('I will bring your guts into your mouth, but that goodness will not die for me!'), but the two meet in his eloquent speech to Hale with its vivid imagery ('Is the accuser always holy now? Were they born this morning as clean as God's fingers?') and in the final speech of this act: 'We are only what we always were, but naked now'. In the same way it is on his three highly-charged and emotive speeches that Act Three ends, and his last speech in the play (already discussed) strikes the moral keynote and the rhetorical high point of the play.

Discussion of character should always involve this range of reference, and should be reinforced by this kind of specific quotation. It should, of course, also pay attention to what is said about the character by the other characters, how they behave towards him, and what effect he has on them. Often, and particularly in the case of *The Crucible*, the author will himself have made some observations about the character and these should also be taken into account.

In the discussion of specimen questions that follows it has been taken for granted that some will suggest themselves automatically and do not need specifying: for example, 'Discuss the character of John Proctor and his role in the play'; 'To what extent and in what ways does Miller engage our sympathy for Abigail?'; 'Compare and contrast Danforth and Hathorne'; or 'In what ways does the character of Hale change as the play develops?'. Answers to all these questions, and to a number of others posed in the course of the critical commentary, have already been suggested in outline.

Once you have defined each character for yourself in this way you can move with greater confidence to the question of how they relate to each other, not only in the action of the play but thematically as well. Try to see them, that is, as individuals, as part of their community, but above all, remembering that they are the fictional creatures of a dramatist's imagination, try to see how they fit in to the overall pattern of the play. In Part 3 many of the main points made about the characters arose out of the discussion of the themes and the structure of the play. Only after that, and then only briefly, were they summed up individually. This was deliberate: the analysis of individual characters is a necessary and relatively straightforward exercise, but one that, like these notes, is of use only to the extent that it leads you to a better perspective on and understanding of the play as a whole. The specimen questions that follow are similarly designed to help in this direction.

The author and his work

Miller has himself commented extensively on this play, on the circumstances in which it came to be written, and on his own attitudes towards it. Illuminating as this information is, the reader must be very careful how he uses it. In recent years D.H. Lawrence's maxim, 'Never trust the artist: trust the tale', has been quoted until it is in danger of becoming a cliché, but only because of its essential truth. What an artist says about his work is always worth listening to but is not to be accepted as beyond dispute. If it does not conform to the impression that the work itself leaves on the reader, the reader should not be afraid of challenging the writer's view, provided that he does so responsibly.

It has already been suggested that in *The Crucible* the artist and the tale differ significantly over the importance of Abigail. Miller's statement that his interest in the story arose from his interest in Abigail's role in it must be accepted as fact: it is, however, legitimate to question whether the play as we have it implies some change of interest on his part during its composition. Similarly, his views on the deliberate malice of the judges were called into question in Part 3. Two questions may be formulated: 'How far does the role of Abigail in the play accord with what Miller's comments in the Introduction lead us to expect?', and 'Compare Miller's comments on the evil of the prosecutors with the impression created by those characters in the play'. Views on both have already been indicated in the notes, but the reader should not accept them unquestioningly and should himself look for further evidence.

The central critical issue here could be focused in the question 'Does Miller's commentary on *The Crucible* help or hinder our understanding of the play?'. Again, the answer must lie with the reader, but he should reach it along the following lines. First, of what does Miller's commentary consist? A distinction should be made between his elucidation of the historical background to the play, his account of his intentions in writing it, and the analogies he draws with the 1950s. Another distinction should be drawn between his more generalised comments (in the Introduction, the Historical Note, and the 'background essay') and his specific comments on individual characters (Putnam and Corey, for example) interpolated in the text. The passage accompanying Hale's first appearance in Act One should then be examined with particular care because that is at one and the same time general and specific, background comment and character description. Having categorised the material in this way the reader should then consider how useful he himself has found each kind of commentary. He should also point to any instances of apparent contradiction between commentary and text, indicating whether he sees these as a source of confusion or as a stimulus to further thought about the play. He ought also to consider whether what, in the long term, helps our *understanding* of the play necessarily contributes to our *enjoyment* of it on first acquaintance.

Another parallel question is 'By what means and with what success does Miller try to make *The Crucible* interesting to the reader as distinct from the audience?'. Much of the same material would have to be considered in answering this, for his commentaries are designed for this purpose also. In addition, some discussion of the stage directions is necessary (in what ways, for example, they go beyond simple instructions to the actor). Some awareness should also be shown of the problems of reading in the study what is designed for performance in the theatre. This too has been touched on already, but again it is for you to form your own opinions.

Society and the individual

Many of Miller's own statements about the play can form the basis of questions and should be looked at in that way. For example, 'Miller has said of *The Crucible* that "the central impulse for writing it at all was not the social but the interior psychological question": to what extent, in your opinion, does the play reflect this?'. The first step is, if possible, to locate the source of the quotation (this comes, in fact, from page 42 of the Introduction to *Collected Plays*) and to see what help, if any, its context gives you in understanding its implications. This question resolves itself into another already discussed: is it a play about Salem or a play about the Proctors? There is, of course, no need to see the alternatives as mutually exclusive, and it may be appropriate to conclude that it encompasses both but in differing proportions. You might also suggest that the impulse seems to have been as much moral as social or psychological. In any case, relate your answer as closely as you can to the text (including the discarded scene), pointing to relevant incidents and quoting appropriate speeches.

A related question is 'What impression does the play give of Salem in 1692?', or, in a more sophisticated form, 'In what ways and with what success does Miller convey in *The Crucible* a sense of a larger community outside the immediate circle of the characters involved?'. Here the starting point could usefully be the Historical Note which promises to convey only 'the essential nature' of the events; this should be reinforced by reference to the statement (again at page 42 of the Introduction) that the difficulty of dramatising the Salem story lay in the large number of characters vitally involved in it; that he had considered, as a dramatic method, 'a mosaic of seemingly disconnected scenes' so as 'to approach the town impressionistically', but had preferred to focus on three characters. Nevertheless, the cast list names twenty-one characters in all; these range from the very young to the very old, from the rich to the poor, from the highest (Danforth) to the lowest (Tituba), and in addition to their part in the action these characters have also a representative role as members of the community. Other people are talked about but not brought on to the stage (Ruth Putnam and Proctor's sons, for example); we hear of events that have taken place in the past or in other towns such as Andover; the characters quarrel over land ownership and other everyday matters; public issues are mentioned (the terms of Parris's appointment, and the factions for and against him); reference is made to the cycle of farming life as the seasons pass, and so on. The opening scene of Act Four must also be discussed in this context (see page 48).

Developing from these topics, of course, is a larger, more philosophical, question: 'What has *The Crucible* to tell us about the relationship between the individual and society?'. Although this moves the issue on to the moral plane, it involves some of the points just discussed. Here it would be well to distinguish between what the play shows the relationship to have been in these historical circumstances and what it implies that the relationship might be. It depicts a society inimical to the individual who will not conform slavishly to whatever society demands: it implies a relationship in which the views of the responsible, principled individual should be listened to more quickly and more constructively. Two associated factors here are the significance of the play's ending (however the reader wishes to interpret it) and the implications of some of Miller's comments outside the play (notably at pages 40–5, 228–9, and 248–50 of *Collected Plays*) on the limited possibilities of social progress. In considering such a question it should also be remembered that we need not expect a dramatist to make an original contribution to social philosophy: it is enough if he highlights responsibly for us the issues that are involved.

The mood of the play

The direction in which the discussion is now moving leads to one final area of questions central to the play's effect: 'Is *The Crucible* too much concerned with ideas and too little concerned with people?'; 'Is *The Crucible* too static and too much of a debate to be theatrically successful?'; 'In *The Crucible* does Miller the intellectual take precedence over Miller the dramatist?'. The discussion in the earlier sections of this book have suggested that the play strikes a successful balance between these two elements, but not all critics would agree with this and there is no reason why the reader should. In answering questions such as these, both sides must be looked at: Miller obviously *is* concerned with ideas, but he also takes definable measures to humanise his characters, to introduce moments of physical action into the play, and to sustain tension and surprise. Even if you believe he should have done more, be sure to give credit for what he has done, and identify it clearly in your answer.

A more difficult variant of these questions is 'Consider the criticism that *The Crucible* is a cold, dispassionate play'. It covers much of the same ground as the other questions, but necessitates fuller discussion of the role of passion and sex in the play. Is Miller's presentation of Elizabeth too much in line with Proctor's criticism of her as cold and aloof? What would the play have gained (or lost) if Proctor's rejection of Abigail had necessitated a greater struggle on his part, and if that struggle had been embodied in the action? (Again the discarded scene has to be taken into account as a pointer). Against this it may be argued that the play has a moral fervour that is anything but cold and dispassionate, that it exhibits the heat of anger if not of love, and that the witchcraft theme introduces a powerful emotive undercurrent.

Finally the language of the play demands attention in this context, as well as providing the basis for other questions such as 'How justifiable is it to complain that the language of *The Crucible* is insufficiently imaginative and too close to the idiom of everyday life?'. The only way of answering this is to identify and discuss the devices by which Miller tries to lift the language above that in daily use: the archaic flavour he gives it (see pages 16-17); the use of vivid and original imagery (Hale's phrase in Act Two, for example: 'If Rebecca Nurse be tainted, then nothing's left to stop the whole green world from burning'); and the use of rhetoric (Hale's great, if partially misguided, speech in Act Three, 'Let you not mistake your duty . . .', should be closely examined). Attention should also be called to the way in which Proctor's speeches at the end of Acts Two, Three, and Four raise the emotional tone of the play. A close analysis of his speech in Act Two ('If *she* be innocent . . .') could show how skilfully Miller utilises repetition and unexpected turns of phrase to vitalise the most ordinary vocabulary into a powerful dramatic utterance. Such speeches, of course, without needing to be numerous, gain in impact by their contrast with the simple directness of the general level of the dialogue which should itself not be underrated. The language constantly reminds us that this is a play about ordinary people in extraordinary circumstances, people whose lives are unexpectedly touched by high drama, and who show themselves able to rise convincingly, but not over-heroically, to its demands.

The Crucible, in short, is a play of great richness, more complex and more evocative than it may at first seem, restrained and yet powerful, and proceeding from an intensity of conviction on the part of its author. Above all, it is a play that calls for, and rewards, close study along the lines that these notes suggest and along others that will doubtless occur to the alert reader.

Part 5

Suggestions for further reading

The text

The text used in these *Notes* has been that of Arthur Miller, *Collected Plays*, Viking Press, New York, 1957; Cresset Press, London, 1958. Reference has also been made to the text printed in *Theatre Arts*, New York, October 1953.

Other plays by Arthur Miller

An Enemy of the People (an adaptation of the play by Henrik Ibsen), Viking Press, New York, 1951.

After the Fall, Viking Press, New York, 1964; Secker & Warburg, London, 1965.

Incident at Vichy, Viking Press, New York, 1965; Secker & Warburg, London, 1966.

The Price, Viking Press, New York, & Secker & Warburg, London, 1968.

The Creation of the World, and Other Business, Viking Press, New York, 1973.

General reading

Historical background

HANSEN, CHADWICK: *Witchcraft at Salem*, George Braziller, New York, 1969.

MARSHALL, CYRIL LEEK: *The Mayflower Destiny*, Stackpole Press, Harrisburg, Pennsylvania, 1975.

STARKEY, MARION L.: *The Devil in Massachusetts*, Knopf, New York, 1949.

Biographical and critical studies

FERRES, JOHN H., (ED.): *Twentieth Century Interpretations of The Crucible*, Prentice-Hall, Englewood Cliffs, New Jersey, 1972. This contains nineteen essays on the play by different authors as well as the text of the discarded scene.

CORRIGAN, ROBERT W., (ED.): *Arthur Miller: a Collection of Critical Essays*, (Twentieth Century Views Series), Prentice-Hall, Englewood Cliffs, New Jersey, 1969. This reprints nine essays by different authors on Arthur Miller, including two specifically on *The Crucible*; it also includes a critical introduction and a bibliography of primary and secondary material.

WELLAND, DENNIS: *Arthur Miller*, (Writers and Critics Series) Oliver & Boyd, Edinburgh and London, 1961. The first full-length monograph to be published on Arthur Miller's work. It has been revised for publication as *Miller: A Study of his Plays*, Eyre Methuen, London, 1979.

The author of these notes

DENNIS WELLAND has taught English at the University of Nottingham; in 1952-1953 he held a Rockefeller Fellowship in the University of Minnesota, returning to set up at Nottingham one of the first British programmes in American Studies. He subsequently became Professor of American Literature in the University of Manchester. He has also taught English and American literature at Indiana University and Amherst College, Massachusetts.

In 1967 he became the founder editor of the *Journal of American Studies* and occupied the post for ten years. In 1974 he edited and contributed to *The USA: A Companion to American Studies,* Methuen, London. He has published articles and reviews on American literary topics in learned journals.

He has also written *Wilfred Owen: A Critical Study*, Chatto & Windus, London, 1960; revised edition, 1978. His most recent book is *Mark Twain in England*, Chatto & Windus, London, 1978.